Free *to* Receive

Become Your True Self by Knowing
What to Accept...and What to Release

DAWNA HETZLER

Cover design by Kristen Ingebretson
Cover photograph copyright © Shutterstock
Author photo by Tammy Marsini, copyright © 2022. All rights reserved.
ND logo: Copyright © New Dawn Companies Inc.

ISBN: 979-8-9867882-1-0 (print)

Printed in the United States of America
First Edition

10 9 8 7 6 5 4 3 2 1

To my Jericho Girls who've climbed with me.

And to the counselors and therapists—the reconciliationists—
who reroute thoughts and create new pathways,
mend hearts and relationships,
and most importantly,
teach us how to receive ourselves.

Miryam opened her heart and received:

Miryam said, "I am the servant of ADONAI; may it happen to me as you have said." Then the angel left her.

—Luke 1:38 (Complete Jewish Bible)

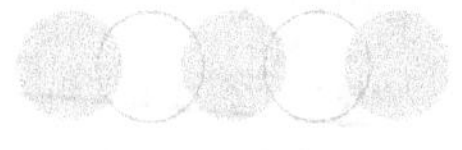

With cheerful expectancy, knowing what you ask is granted to the extent I'm open to receive!

—Russell Dennis

Contents

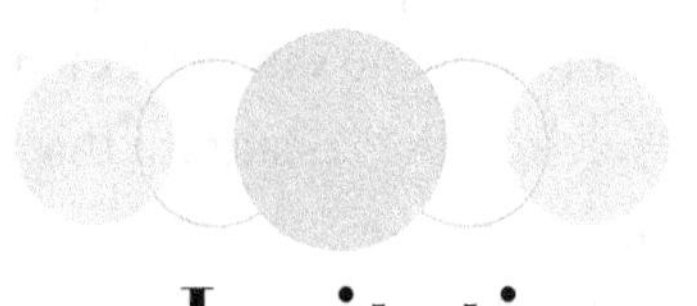

an Invitation

MOST OF US REALIZE WE'RE FAR FROM OUR TRUE SELVES. We're carrying around a lot of unwanted baggage, and at times, we expect others to carry it for us.

We receive the wrong things and reject the right things.

The result is that we've lowered our expectations of what's possible. And many feel too worn out, embarrassed, or disqualified to keep trying.

It's easy to get lost circling unproductive paths, but you don't always have to succumb to that process.

What if I told you that simple tiny adjustments and filtering what you take into your mind, heart, and soul can help you find a new path?

In 2008, I entered what I call a "lonely desert season," which led me to step up financially and emotionally in ways I never thought possible or felt capable of. In one long decade, I retraced areas I knew weren't working.

Just when I thought I'd found my way out of the desert, I discovered I was at the base of an emotional mountain God was asking me to climb, and I didn't want to make the trek. When 2017 rolled around, I'd completely lost myself and the life I once thought was so great.

How had I become so disconnected from myself and those whom I love?

I'd met a friend for lunch who was older than me and absolutely gorgeous. As I walked into the restaurant that day, she appeared even more beautiful.

So, I said to her, "You look stunning!"

Her response was, "Oh honey, it's just the lighting."

While I should've taken this as her typical humble response, her words made me pause.

How many times had I rejected simple kindness that I should've accepted?

The question lingered with me. After our lunch date, my heart searched deeper. How had my life been shaped by what I received and rejected? So, I embarked on a journey to learn more.

I not only discovered how hard it was for most of us to receive even something as simple as a compliment, but I also found that receiving well is healthy and blocking the unhealthy is vital. We tend to do the opposite, though: reject the good and absorb the bad. What we open or close ourselves to impacts our lives and shapes the person we're becoming.

We miss opportunities to live fully because we simply can't take from others. We tend to live by the mantra, "It is more blessed to give than to receive," (Acts 20:35 [New International Version]), but it's not always easy to *receive*. Not being open to receiving from others hinders us from things like accepting a gift, taking in helpful criticism, or asking for help. Often, it becomes painful to accept from someone. But being sons and daughters of God means that whether it's help we need, advice we seek, or asking a friend to hold up the mirror of truth, we must be able to receive.

Additionally, we need to reject that which isn't good for us. Knowing and owning what *not* to receive is just as important. Learning to do so teaches us how to completely accept ourselves and helps us become the person we want to be.

I discovered there were some things I shouldn't allow into my mind, heart, and soul and some I should've invited in but didn't. I also learned I needed to open up to elements I didn't want to—like truths that I needed to hear but didn't want to face.

I began to understand who I was. Changing wrong narratives by debunking childhood chronicles taught me to trust and love myself. I experienced God's ultimate goodness and started accepting it fully. And once I was strong enough, I slowly opened my heart to the kindness of others and unknowingly discovered the principle of receiving.

My life was changing for the better, and I felt empowered to find my authentic self. There's freedom in letting go, accepting, and completely receiving, whether it's from yourself, God, or another person. Learning to do so split the atmosphere of my life, and I stepped into a new way of *being.* I began to focus on what *I* could change, and the only real thing I could change was me.

But you can change your circumstances too. You're not helpless or "blown about by the wind." When you focus on improving yourself, everyone and everything has to either step up to the new level you've attained or stay put. And while working on yourself, you'll become rooted enough to make strong decisions and strengthened to face any outcome.

I invite you to journey with me. Pick up your backpack, trek through a desert, climb a mountain, and uncover the truth about receiving goodness. I'm hoping that through my story, you'll discover what I did—a better way to know what truly matters and how to live from that place.

We'll discover childhood giants. We'll explore wrong narratives and how to make them right again. And together, we'll see that we can be open to goodness and shut down what's not.

There are seven principles to apply to your life that will open your heart to more:

1. learning to hone and trust your own intuition;
2. dropping the weight of things you aren't meant to carry;
3. looking deeply into your heart's motivation and fine-tuning it;
4. discovering, welcoming, honoring, and managing those who sit around your inner table;
5. understanding when to open and close your heart;
6. creating a breathable and flexible list to help you live freely; and
7. accepting within after all that's transpired in your life with God and others.

Everything that comes to us is not equal. Whether our circumstances are different or the same, we can learn how to live our best lives.

To become your true self, you must learn what and how to receive…and not receive.

Together, we'll reach the summit and make it back down the mountain, radiant and shining with new glory.

Will you make the climb with me?

Part One

A Life of Receiving the Wrong Things

1

Little Girl Lost

If I have seen further than others,
it is by standing upon the shoulders of giants.
— Isaac Newton

MASHED POTATOES.

Trivial, right? Yet, one simple bowl of potatoes led to half a lifetime of inadequacy.

I stood on the kitchen chair to reach my workstation. Elevated and seeing from a new viewpoint, I whipped up my creation. The wind of independence blew from the back of the electric mixer and swooshed through my hair. I was just a little girl, but I was creating a huge masterpiece.

Turning the power button to the off position, I ran my finger around the inside of the bowl to clean up the splatter. I tasted it, and it was good. With a huge smile, I turned to face Mama for approval.

Mama's indifference cut to my heart. "They're still lumpy."

I turned to re-whip them and make it right, but before I could, Mama said something else.

"Let your cousin do it. She won't leave lumps."

Hurt buckled my legs and forced me to a kneeling position on the chair. So disappointed, I didn't realize I'd left the kitchen until I was in the next room. All I knew was that what I'd created wasn't enough.

I was too young to understand what took residency in my heart at that very moment. I wasn't capable of comprehending how it would shape me—feeling inadequate and accepting blame from others when in reality, I didn't do anything wrong.

Embarrassed and wounded, I thought, *How did I mess that up?*

At dinner, I'd lost my appetite as I moved bite-sized pieces of meat and vegetables around my plate under the sad pile of potatoes.

I'd received the wrong message. Maybe my mashed potatoes weren't so bad, and my mama just needed efficiency.

If I look back with a nonemotional glance, maybe it was a case of repeated family patterns. My grandmother, Neva, had served in the US Army and ran her household like the military. While Neva was an amazing grandmother and my superhero, she was especially hard on my mother and her two sons. That militant style might've spilled into my mom's own parenting. But regardless of the *why*, this little girl's heart needed love, nurturing, and affirmation; instead, tough parenting led me to believe I was inadequate.

The simplest things leave scars that we carry with us into adulthood. I call them "childhood giants." These emerge from emotional events that shape our perceptions. I spent the majority of my life fighting three of these beasts: *never good enough, abandoned,* and *carrying blame.*

My mashed potato experience created a giant that taunted me into thinking I couldn't do anything right. Because of this creature, I lived way too many years striving for perfection. I falsely believed that if I could do things correctly, I'd receive the love and affirmation I needed. Someone would certainly come along and say, "You created a masterpiece. I love your potatoes."

Another battle I faced was *abandonment.*

This monster took hold of me as a child when my cousin ditched me at a horse racing track. I was lost and couldn't find my parents, and I started to panic until a stranger helped me find my family. Although reunited, the fear of not being with my mom and dad took over and led me to believe I could run from this giant if I tried hard enough to overcome it.

"I can do it" became my motto.

If I could care for myself, it would certainly alleviate the fear of being left on my own.

Except subconsciously, I was still scared to be alone—not as in alone time, but to be deserted by those I love. It wasn't until much later when someone actually walked out of my life that I realized I'm all right on my own. I discovered that I'm more than capable of caring for myself. There's been no better life lesson for me than to face my giants head-on. When thrown into one of my biggest fears, I found that the taunting was more terrifying than actually facing it.

The third childhood giant I fought was *carry the blame.*

I discovered that as a little girl, I wasn't free to express my opinion without some type of consequence. If I was afraid, someone in my family would tell me why I shouldn't be.

"How can you be scared of *that*?"

If I needed to talk about something deep or important, I'd be redirected from my feelings.

"Come on, let's go have some fun. Let's quit all this serious talk."

I went into shutdown mode. I felt bad for trying to approach deep topics or share my feelings. So, I'd carry the blame, thinking I did or said something wrong when in reality I didn't. Ultimately, I hadn't found my own true voice.

As I grew up, my *not good enough, abandoned,* and *carry the blame* giants taunted me even louder. I unknowingly fought them in unproductive ways, but I didn't know they existed as clearly as I describe them now or how to overcome them.

One statement from someone close was all it took for me to suddenly feel insufficient, even when it wasn't meant that way. In someone's anger, I'd discover myself trying to extinguish it because I didn't want to be left alone. And without a clear voice, I'd convince myself I'd done something wrong and would carry someone else's problem. Eventually, I began doubting myself and embracing that which wasn't mine to hold.

These childhood experiences shaped a false reality of who I was and how I responded to life situations, and I spent too much of my adult life like that. I hadn't realized it was all inside me and stemmed from a past that rendered me not good enough, abandoned, and responsible for other's words and actions.

Without realizing it, I'd overexplain myself when I felt "I didn't mash the potatoes properly." When an argument arose, I'd try to extinguish it quickly for fear I'd be left alone. And when trying to express my feelings or opinions, if someone didn't agree or challenged me, I felt my arms reaching out to carry their ideas, values, or feelings instead of my own.

When those giants came out to bully me, my brain slowed down to the point where I could hardly think.

In those situations, logic eluded me. I call it "mind mire" (MM).

Mind Mire

When you place beaters into a too-thick mixture, the beaters decelerate. The motor isn't strong enough to "move around the sludge" and begins to smell like burning metal. That's what it seemed like when I'd mentally seize up—thoughts wouldn't come, and I could almost smell my words smoldering. My brain would literally get stuck, and I physically couldn't speak.

When questioned, "Why did you do that?" I couldn't think of a reason. If someone didn't support one of my achievements, I went right back to being the little girl in that chair holding the mixer. Frozen in my responses, I wouldn't be able to articulate my thoughts, and if I could explain, what I said sounded foolish.

I'd second-guess myself, and all I would hear was that *I* was at fault or that *I* was not good enough.

Trying to reason that my mashed potatoes *weren't lumpy*, I worked hard to make sure I was a superwoman. I was a fabulous cook; I exercised to look my best; I worked hard to demonstrate my success; I went to college…

There was nothing I wouldn't try just to prove myself, so I became everything for everyone. *I can do it!*

But no matter how much I accomplished, I needed more to fuel my self-worth.

And while I was more than capable of doing many things at once, I eventually discovered that I didn't need to prove my abilities. This happened years later during my emotional mountain climb. I was pushing too hard, and I needed rest. In my weariness, I finally said, "This overdoing is stupid!" When I finally allowed myself the grace of an exhale, I remembered that God requires us to let up and slow down, inviting us to take a pause with Him. In doing so, I gently let go of the past and of striving. I learned to open up to receive God's reflection of who I truly am. I saw that I *could* do it, but I didn't *need* to.

I began learning about what was physically happening when I'd experience MM. When the fight-or-flight mechanism is triggered, it inhibits the part of the brain that deals with logic, decision-making, and formulating responses.[1] Instead of fight or flight, my brain locked up. While the adrenaline-induced fight or flight is a God-designed safety mechanism critical for survival, it wasn't serving me well emotionally.

I started working through what I could do to settle down and think logically in the midst of emotional moments. First, when I'd feel the threat of confrontation and the perceived threat of abandonment, my thoughts would slow, so I'd tell the other person I needed to pause and return to the conversation later.

Leaving the discussion and actually walking away helped create some much-needed space in order to discover what was triggering MM. Once I'd had time to think, breathe, and identify my giant, logical thinking returned, and I was better able to articulate a response.

Removing myself from a heated conversation was a healthy decision. Staying could lead me to believe I did something wrong even when I hadn't. As I practiced settling down, clear thinking returned, and voicing my position came quicker. Once logic came back, I was able to revisit the conversation and communicate my thoughts properly. This helped my brain get out of the MM and recover faster.

As I developed this skill, I was able to remain in uncomfortable conversations that provoked my *not good enough, abandonment,* and *carry the blame* childhood giants. Now more skilled at dealing with this issue, I'm able to stay connected rather than leave to recover my thinking.

Another practice that was helpful was diverting my mind when I would feel MM coming on; I could think of happy thoughts and other things that would soothe me.

---

1. Arlin Cuncic, "Amygdala Hijack and the Fight or Flight Response," Very Well Mind, last modified June 22, 2021, https://www.verywellmind.com/what-happens-during-an-amygdala-hijack-4165944.

After this, I'm going to get ice cream. I love ice cream.

Reminding myself of the things I love to do—like get a massage or take a drive—helped keep my brain from seizing up.

This distraction method kept me more focused on the good, and eventually, my MM became less severe. My logical brain recovered quicker, and I could more readily identify what I needed in each situation without leaving.

There were also times when my mind went on overload and reacted out of anger. I typically let things build for too long without expressing my thoughts and emotions.

The same mechanism was at work here—fight or flight took over from logic. The only difference was that I was irrational, and that type of response always led to trouble. So, I kept practicing the techniques I learned to be present in confrontation and react beneficially.

Childhood giants come to life through our experiences and perceptions of the world around us. Just like the messages I'd accepted growing up, I received the wrong story.

Even a compliment can be taken the wrong way, like the time I was told, "I love the wrinkles around your eyes when you laugh."

I thought, *I have eye wrinkles?*

Once I became aware of them, I thought of myself as getting older. From there, I only saw the wrinkles around my eyes and not the laughter that put them there.

What about your childhood?

What's your mashed potato story?

Childhood giants want to harm us and teach us to receive the wrong things. They want the little girl on the inside to be lost.

While we could stand on their shoulders to see farther, ultimately, we'd still be fighting them. We can't climb them to get a better viewpoint; they have to be slayed. And together, we will learn to slay these giants.

But before I was able to combat my own giants, another war waged in my adult life.

2

Grown-up Problems
and Pretending

We are what we pretend to be,
so we must be careful about what we pretend to be.
—Kurt Vonnegut, *Mother Night*

LIFE ISN'T AS SIMPLE WHEN YOU'RE OLDER AND WISER AS WHEN you're young and naive.

I thought my husband, David, and I had turned the corner after almost a decade of financial and emotional crises, and I falsely believed we made it through an extremely difficult journey. After all, he'd acted as if things were improving. Everything he said he needed, I worked desperately to give him—up until the night of our talk. I had told myself, "We made it through. It was tough, and we have scars, but we made it."

But that night in December 2017, he said in his despair, "I'm feeling disconnected from you."

My heart sank into a pit. *Was he still in love with me?*

A lot transpired between 2008 and 2017.

We were always a team. High school sweethearts and working together professionally for many years—he built homes, and I sold them. We had it all, and though we never would've admitted it, we needed nothing and no one but each other.

Disaster struck in 2008. We experienced such loss that when we fell apart, I thought I would crumble.

David had just finished building two high-end houses. We'd owned many other homes, land, and investments and were working hard to create a good life and maybe even retire early. Our world had been carefully planned and constructed through much toil and digging. And then, at the pinnacle of our success, the economy collapsed.

Everything we worked for disappeared overnight. Two decades of praying and striving slid like sand through our fingers, and all we could do was watch it go. As with so many others, in the blink of an eye, our net worth became a fraction of what it'd once been. And as the recession stretched into months, David began losing his sense of identity and the confidence to lead our family.

The worst part wasn't losing the money but watching my husband slip away. Defeat lined his face, and I could see his spirit become overwhelmed. Nothing I did or said helped him recover.

By 2010, my husband had morphed into someone I barely recognized. Honestly, I thought he was going to die. If not physically, then spiritually. Stress ate over forty pounds from him, and fear aged his face. But what scared me the most was how he disconnected himself from me and his life. David had given up, and I tried everything I could think of to bring him back from his desolate isolation.

I pressed on for ten years, striving to keep us afloat. I'd lost my home and retirement fund and emotionally lost my husband. As he withdrew from life, I felt the responsibility fall on my shoulders. But like raking water uphill, my solitary efforts were largely futile. It was me against the world—alone.

I wouldn't allow myself to receive help because if I did, it might reveal my need. Remember, *I can do it!* was the motto I used to fight my giants.

But I wasn't ready to face my reality. Not yet.

I just tried everything I could to get David's head back in the game in hopes he'd partner with me again.

We were a great team up until the world broke us apart.

I just wanted my world right again—and he was my world.

I became blinded by my own fantasy. What I discovered was that I wouldn't take an honest look at my life so I could keep my anxiety at a manageable level. As frightened as I was to face the facts, without admitting it, I knew we emerged from our journey disconnected and injured.

● ● ●

Our woundedness began in our childhood years and followed us into our relationship. Perhaps I started pretending when I slinked down from the chair and out of the kitchen after attempting to make mashed potatoes, thinking, *Mama's words don't hurt.*

Maybe it was after I got home from the horse racing track and discovered how quickly I could become separated, thinking, *I'm not scared to be alone.*

Or it could've been the time in between trying to find my own voice only to have it shut down, taking the blame for things that weren't mine to carry.

Regardless, I learned false pretense. "I'm fine."

Married as young adults, there were times David and I couldn't clearly communicate to each other what we really needed. Or if we did, the other would hear something totally dissimilar. For example,

I'd realized our definitions of *protection* were distinctly different: I focused on physical protection from him while he looked at emotional protection from me. This led to us treating each other poorly at times.

Alexander Milov's sculpture, *Love*,[2] is a rebar sculpture of a man and a woman sitting back-to-back with their shoulders slumped in anguish and despair. Inside each rebar statue is a little boy and a little girl aglow with hands outstretched attempting to reunite. It reminded me of how deeply our child within desperately longs to connect. An impactful image of where David and I were and, unfortunately, where many of us find ourselves in our relationships.

We didn't discover this until much deeper into our relationship, and that contributed to our disconnect. What we later learned was that these issues bound us so tightly, it rendered us "emotionally fused" and caused greater distance between us.

But neither of us could see what was happening—we were too close to the situation. And if I dared to look, I might've seen that we were falling apart and facing defeat. But I wouldn't be defeated. Not by this or by anything.

Yet it came, ready or not. I sat there in dismay as David told me he was unhappy in our marriage. Thoughts and emotions flooded me as my heart sank into utter disbelief while feelings of hurt, ungratefulness, and anger emerged.

I thought, *How can this be when I've worked so diligently to help him?*

I wouldn't look at the fact that I'd contributed to that moment too. I wasn't ready to confront myself and see that I had to take responsibility for my half of the muck.

---

2. Alexander Milov, *Love*, 2015, Ukraine, Love Milov, accessed May 4, 2022, http://milova.net/love.

I didn't know how, and I didn't want to face myself.

That night in December of 2017, somewhere in the long stretch between Christmas and the New Year, I felt myself slipping into my darkest place.

Where had it all gone wrong?

How could things shift so drastically after striving for so long to keep it all together?

But there wasn't a drastic shift; it had been a slow eroding that revealed our hearts of stone. We'd betrayed ourselves and were deceived by the enemy of our souls. We'd taken each other for granted, hated parts of the other, and despised ourselves.

There was still hope, though, because hate isn't the opposite of love—apathy is. We both still cared; we just didn't know if the embers would stay aflame.

As David continued to talk that cold winter night, I felt the sadness of extreme loss. Not only did David lose his identity, I'd lost myself as well. In all my attempts to make life right again—striving, fixing, appeasing, enabling, and encouraging to a fault—I realized that somewhere along the way, he wasn't the only one who'd given up.

I'd given up on us too.

The full impact of our situation bore down on me—so many years gone to waste.

All my futile attempts to make life right laughed in my face. It was pointless; all of my proud moments of carrying us through life's battles were lying on the floor, mocking me in my pain.

I took a hard look at myself and my contributions to the mess we were in and stared at myself in the eye, trying to decide who I wanted to be and who I wanted to be with. I'd avoided it for too long, and it landed me there.

We need to look at and pay attention to who we're morphing into.

Not facing ourselves will quickly build a wall around the heart, shielding and hiding in hopes we don't have to look deep within.

Pretending stops us from receiving the truths God requires us to face. He wants us to become sons and daughters who receive what He's laid out for us: *life on God's terms.* He calls us to a relationship with Him so we can experience His peace in the midst of the storm.

Not taking a true look at myself served me in many ways, but not for the better. The "pretending" I'm referring to makes the individual smaller. In doing so, I didn't have to acknowledge that I repeated dysfunctional family patterns I swore I'd never do, like making my husband feel less than, enabling him, or not coming to his rescue the way he needed when the world turned on him.

If I would've stopped my false acting, I wouldn't have lost my way. This wasn't so easy, though, because David is the most important person in my life. Taking a truthful look at our situation would've forced me to see that we aren't invincible, and I love the notion that we are. So, I falsely believed he was getting better, even though he wasn't.

I didn't look at my reality, and while it got me through, it did more damage than good. When I thought it helped me, it actually blocked my ability to receive. I needed to accept our situation so I could step into faith and trust what God was doing in our lives.

Pretending and living by faith are completely different. When I was the financial provider to keep us afloat, I was scared to death. But somehow, dealing with the loss of finances was an easier act of faith. I didn't pretend we were financially okay. I looked at the situation squarely and said, "God, I will do everything in my power, but ultimately, it's You who will lead us out of this."

This bold act of faith turned me into a strong and successful businesses woman; something that hiding from the situation never would've done.

Have you dodged yourself by putting on false pretenses?

It's easier not to look and more comfortable to recline in the familiar.

Truth be told, I was cozy in my emotional hypocrisy. I didn't want to see because if I truly examined myself, I would've discovered I'd played a part, and *I* needed to change too. And what if in the process of my changes, David and I didn't fit together anymore?

I had to stop my attempts to fix David's life and figure out how to fix my own.

What I didn't know then was that the only broken thing I could repair was within, but I couldn't fix what I didn't know or didn't want to see.

I had to stop pretending and blaming everyone else for what my life had become. I had to receive things about myself I never had the courage to look at before. It was my opportunity to receive what I didn't want to and truly look hard at myself and who I was.

It was painful. I'd believed that I had it all figured out, but in hindsight, I was a mess.

I entered therapy for the first time in my life. I went to my sessions initially with the wrong agenda—to change David.

"If only he'd taken control of his life and regained his identity, we wouldn't be here now."

Subtly, my therapist directed our discussions to what I could change in *myself*.

"If you wait for David to change to your liking, you've given him all the power, and no one should have that much power. Instead, let's focus on you. As you begin changing your own dynamics, you'll become empowered to live the life *you* want."

I had no idea how that was supposed to strengthen our marriage, but I trusted and began applying the practices I learned to become the person I wanted to be.

My therapist taught me how to confront myself truthfully and gracefully as I embarked on getting rid of pretense and seeing the real me. I faced childhood giants. I found that I needed to learn to articulate better, fight more productively, understand my feelings, and share them. I had to understand how to take better care of and believe in myself. I faced the fact that I must allow David to discover who he wanted to be without my input or help.

Through that, I started to see that I had a terrible relationship with *myself*. It all seemed too overbearing, but I had no other option. I had to quit putting on a false act.

It saddens me that it's taken almost fifty years to begin to sort out my "stuff" from the impact my childhood experiences had on my adult life and my marriage. While I can't go back and redo that part of my life, I'm grateful to have found out how to work through the things that hindered me.

This new season ushered the greatest lesson of my life: quit pretending and receive all of me—the bad, good, ugly, and beautiful—and then tweak wherever needed.

I also learned a new dimension of receiving from God—how to graciously receive and when to *not* receive from others. A whole new life awaited if I just leaned in.

I was finally discovering the real me, and it was frightening and empowering at the same time. My therapist was right; no one should have more power over you than yourself. That became especially true when I quit pretending and began living with integrity by looking at the real me and working on becoming the person I desired to be.

Life isn't as simple as when we're young and naive.

Failures and disappointments ring a bell that can't be taken back, but those life experiences aren't supposed to be a resonating sound that hinders us. They're meant for something much greater—to shape us into who we were originally created to be.

And that's exactly why we need to examine ourselves closely. We need to be brave enough to peek; the closer we look, the stronger we are to change ourselves for the better.

I stood in front of the mirror of truth. What would I discover?

3

Brave Enough to Peek

If you are out to describe the truth,
leave elegance to the tailor.
—Albert Einstein

I LOST MY TRUEST SELF BY PRETENDING SO I WOULDN'T HAVE TO deal with "messy me" or the arduous work of transformation. Who wants to toil that hard or spend any time looking at all *that*?

It's difficult to climb out of the comforts of a La-Z-Boy recliner to stand in your own anxiety that comes with change. I sat in my rut for years, but the status quo stunted my hero within.

It takes bravery to even peek at oneself.

With an honest look, it's possible to break free from familiar, non-productive cycles. Deciding to evaluate myself initiated from hardship and a feeble attempt to be brave.

There's typically a catalyst that forces the peek, though. My unease came at the end of 2017 when it felt like my world was completely unraveling. I was super uncomfortable with my life at that point, so I peeked. I noticed some things within me I didn't like and decided I wanted more for myself.

I want to articulate the truths I discovered about myself gracefully, but truth isn't always elegant, and nobody learns from perfection. As I tried to see my shortcomings, I realized I had a daunting list.

I was emotionally dependent.

I never learned to identify, validate, or articulate my feelings.

I lived in fear of confrontation.

I enabled by fixing.

I risked my own integrity in order to be liked.

And I'd lived life believing other's opinions instead of believing in my own.

Once I recognized these traits, among others, I was immediately overwhelmed. Where would I begin? And what would the outcomes be?

If I changed my dependency and learned to stand on my own emotionally, would my marriage fall apart?

If I stopped pushing myself and began listening to my innermost feelings, would I become an empath? Or, on the other end of the spectrum, self-absorbed?

If I confronted situations and people who weren't healthy in my life, would I lose those relationships?

What kind of person would I become if I stopped "helping" and quit jeopardizing my own integrity in order to be liked?

What would it feel like to trust myself?

As I asked myself these questions, I felt the fear of the unknown. Despair washed over me as I realized I had to make a choice: stay within the comfort zone of who I knew myself to be, or take a chance on change and a new beginning despite the risks.

As I began to look within, I realized the variable outcomes made me feel like change would bring the death of all I'd known and was important to me.

It felt better to not wake a sleeping giant, but they're only resting for the next battle.

Only one version of myself would emerge: the me who desperately tiptoed around idle giants, or the one who would rise to slay them. I decided to stand and fight.

Once I made that decision, it felt insurmountable just to deal with one of my struggles, let alone all of them. So, I began with the one I wanted to overcome the most—my emotional dependence. I never knew what it meant to completely stand on my own.

I started by peeking—just a quick glance and assessment. Then, I implemented a small change and worked on solely depending on myself emotionally. To take some pressure off, I put no time frame on myself and just observed how my revamping was working. *Was it serving me well?*

I set boundaries with myself and others.

I learned to say, "I can't do that. I don't know why; I just can't."

And I came to terms with various unplanned outcomes and learned to let go of them. It was freeing—an exhale I'd unconsciously craved my whole life. I uncovered a deeper self-integrity I didn't know I carried: the honesty it takes to hold on to the truest and deepest parts of me—trusting my intuition, listening to my sentiments, and speaking to what I feel.

As things shifted inside, a different perspective took over. It became less frightening to look at my life and see it more truthfully. I was loving the person in me who slowly took shape.

As victorious as I was with one self-improvement, I rested before beginning another. Once I felt ready to work on the next, I began taking small peeks at the next issue I wanted to overcome.

While undertaking one thing at a time, I wrestled with how I allowed myself to live in such bondage by being so unaware. Had I wasted all my youthful years because I didn't see myself for who I'd truly become? And most importantly, how would I receive or reject all that transpired in the decade of my desert wilderness years? Complete acceptance wouldn't come for a while, but I was working on it.

I began to feel empowered as positive outcomes took shape. In doing something different, I was able to change *me*, and everyone in my life either came along or stayed behind. Either way, it strengthened me to face whatever happened.

When we look, then we can change. That doesn't mean we won't slip back into old habits, though.

How about you? Have you been brave enough to look at your own life and evaluate what would serve you better? What challenges have held you back from truly examining yourself?

Waffling, Acquiescing, and Standing Firm

I put one small triangle on his plate, then I took it off and hovered, uncertain. My heart was in the right place; after all, this was how I showed love—by giving David more than he asked for. I put the quarter piece of waffle back on his plate and took it off again. For heaven's sake, I was waffling over a waffle!

When I began making breakfast, I asked David if he wanted hash browns or waffles. He said he wanted hash browns, but I wanted waffles, so I made both, which left me with the dilemma of whether or not to give him a waffle, too. As I said, I believed giving more meant loving more.

In the past, that wouldn't have been an issue. I would've simply given him both hash browns and a waffle, and he'd receive it even if he didn't want it, and we'd continued on with breakfast.

Except everything was different.

The last few years, we'd been working on the little things in our relationship that eventually became bigger issues—even the seemingly insignificant things like this waffle dilemma. Delivering just hash browns would've been the right thing to do.

I handed him his plate, and David chuckled as he looked at his breakfast. Tears first welled in my heart. I'd failed. I knew the minute I handed it to him that I'd backslid.

"Why bother asking me what I want if you're going to give me whatever *you* want?"

He recognized the unproductive patterns in our relationship more readily than before.

I reached out to take it off his plate, but he pulled back. The tears in my heart made their way to my cheeks.

"Why are you crying, Dawni?"

David's called me that sweet nickname ever since we were kids and uses it when he tends to me.

"It's just that…well…I love you, and I want you to feel like I give you *more* than you ask for. And while I know it's just a stupid waffle, I've learned enough through our journey that these little things we do add up to bigger issues. I'm not sure of the bigger issue right now, but I know I'm finding comfort in old ways."

I cried. David was gentle with me; he gave me a hug and ate his breakfast. And we continued on with our day.

It's not easy sticking with change; falling back into old patterns is part of the process.

I'd grown enough to recognize that I was finding solace in my familiar ways and wanted to soothe the anxiety of implementing so many new things in our relationship.

All the progress we'd made didn't come effortlessly. I was tired and afraid of the "yet to be seen" outcomes of all the new practices we were experimenting with.

I simply longed for my comforting old routines, if only for a moment over breakfast. Perhaps he, too, was tired of working so hard on himself and our relationship. Without saying another word, we moved on.

Yet, something didn't sit right with me about my actions that morning. The breakfast felt weighted, and because it lingered, I knew it needed to be addressed from within.

Some little things I do can be received negatively, which make David feel patronized or disrespected. If taken that way, the subtle nuances collect like small droplets in a bucket, eventually cascading into resentment.

What was I *truly* waffling over?

David and I were individually transforming for the better, and that was contributing positively to our marriage, but it hadn't been easy. I just needed a break from all the change.

The familiar ease of how we'd navigated our past relationship for so many years felt soothing, even if those ways were less productive than the new ones we'd implemented. It *was* disappointing to see how readily I could fall back into my old habits, though.

I was proud of myself for recognizing that deeper truth, but I was also lying to myself that my reason for giving David more was for him to feel loved. I mean, of course I wanted him to feel loved, but there were other ways to do that without overruling his wishes. Once I overrode what David really wanted (hash browns and not waffles), it was already done. I tried to change my mind after I'd acted, but it was too late—I couldn't take back a waffle.

Aside from finding comfort in my old ways of interacting with David, something felt unsettling with the waffling part—changing my mind—and I wanted to find out why.

Sitting in my therapist's office, I discussed my waffle story. While I wanted to stay in congratulations mode for recognizing my deeper truth, my therapist peeled back more layers.

"In that moment making breakfast, why do you think you overrode David's request and gave him more than he asked for?" my therapist asked me.

"I wanted him to feel loved by giving him abundance."

"How come just serving him the breakfast he ordered wasn't enough?"

"I don't know," I'd said, but I felt my *never good enough* giant lingering in the shadow.

"If David was at a restaurant, would a waitress override his order and give him something he didn't ask for?"

I fidgeted at her question. "No."

Silence sat between us.

"That's why I'm here," I said finally. "Help me so I don't go back to my old patterns—overriding what he wants, searching for validation, and doing and being everything to everyone. I've failed once again. Just like I failed in helping David recover from the downturn."

"You didn't fail. Perhaps you could've done things differently, though."

She let me think on that before she continued.

"Why do you believe it was your sole responsibility to help David recover?"

"I'm his wife. We're supposed to help each other up."

"What if you tried to pick him up but he remained seated? Would you exhaust yourself trying to get him to stand?"

"No." My voice trailed off. "But I did."

"Dawna, it's okay to help your husband, but there comes a point when there's too much assistance. I help my kids with their homework, but if they asked me to do their homework for them, would that be helpful?"

"Of course not. But have you ever stared into the eyes of someone emotionally dying? 'Doing his homework' helped me hold on to hope in our bleak circumstances. It was the only assignment in front of me, and I took it."

"How does that leave you feeling?"

"Frustrated. I now understand that I can't help someone recover—they have to want it for themselves. I'm always *responsible Dawna* who tries to help too much."

"I like *responsible Dawna*. She's resourceful, and she gets things done. What I don't like is when she's 'on' all the time. What would happen if you stopped caring for everyone else and began taking care of you? It seems you haven't taken very good care of *yourself*."

That was an accurate assessment. I'd given so much of myself to others that I didn't realize I was slowly losing myself. I understood the part I played in the struggles of our marriage, but I worked hard for many years to redeem it. In fact, when my efforts didn't amount to anything, I felt like I had nothing left. And perhaps that's the reason I fell so hard.

"Why do you think you need to over-function?"

"That's noteworthy," I said, utilizing one of her lines to show how her "over-function" statement resonated with me.

She continued. "I really like how you've been identifying what you need, owning your voice, and clearly stating it to David. I also like how you recognized that something was off in your waffle-making scenario and you came here to face it. It's good that you're learning and starting to care for yourself while continuing to work on you."

"So, my overdoing things isn't because I love him and want to give him so much?"

"I believe you love him and want to give him the best of you, but doing and being all isn't what's best *for* you."

"I'm afraid."

"Of…?" she asked.

"What happens if in our individual growth, we find that we no longer need each other? What if I grow and he remains the same? What if he outgrows me?"

"That's interesting," she said. "Could this fear drive you to do too much?"

"Yes."

"During the decade where David lost his identity, you said you feared the complete loss of who David once was, as there was reasonable chance he wouldn't return to his old self. If that turned out to be the case, you might lose him altogether. So, you over functioned out of fear. The same thing is happening now. You see good change in you and in David, but there's a possibility of outgrowing the other, and that's frightening."

I was beginning to see the light. I gave him the waffle not because I love him so much (which I do), but more because I was fearful of the unknown outcomes of who we were becoming. To ease that fear, I over functioned and gave too much, falling into old habits for my own comfort.

She continued. "As one person grows, the other is forced to grow alongside them or get left behind. If one doesn't change and develop with their partner, chances are that the relationship will fail. The one who refuses to change, settles for the way things once were—that's why we work so hard in our relationships to keep the status quo. If everyone remains the same, no one risks a breakup."

It all made sense. I was brave enough to peek at myself, but in doing so, I saw that I was waffling—changing my mind because I found comfort in going back instead of pressing on. Changing back to my old self also minimized the risk of outgrowing David or him outgrowing me. If either one of us stepped back into our old tango, it was likely we'd both participate in our dysfunctional dance. So, I over functioned out of fear, and it caused me to do things like give him the waffle he didn't ask for and override his wishes.

By over functioning, I wasn't solidified in who I was, which led to waffling or *changing my mind*. I longed to be a more solid person, but I didn't want the pain of change.

There were deeper truths hidden, and it seemed so overwhelming.

I pondered. *Do I want to continue finding the true me?*

I could lose David. He was all I'd ever known.

I was coming to a new understanding about my own decisions and actions, and I began to change my unhealthy way of operating by acknowledging my fear and speaking to it.

"Yep. In becoming a better version of myself, there's a risk. Whatever the outcome, God will see me through it."

Then I stood firm in my new and strong voice.

In Dr. Lerner's book, *The Dance of Anger,* she boldly proclaimed, "When a woman clarifies the issues and uses her anger to move toward something new and different, then change occurs. If she stops *over functioning* for others and starts acting for herself, her *under functioning* man is likely to acknowledge and deal with his own anxieties."[3]

I was quickly realizing I couldn't possibly be David's or anyone else's everything—only God could be that. God is the only one who can be all and do all without over functioning. He has the ability to love completely *and* the power to let go. He lovingly comes alongside us but doesn't do everything for us.

God is not an over-functioner.

---

3. Harriet Lerner, *The Dance of Anger: A Woman's Guide to Changing the Patterns of Intimate Relationships.* (New York, NY: Harper & Row, 1985), 55.

I also discovered over functioning creates enabling, and enabling stops another person from stepping up. Why would anyone want to take charge when things are being handled for them? Doing too much for others creates disconnect because you can't be intimately connected if you don't allow someone to help *you*. Ultimately, it blocks the ability to receive.

It's been a difficult journey making these lasting changes. I broke old emotional habits that had taken root as a child and grown deep into my adult life. When I let go of outcomes, I more readily received what was best for me. I stopped waffling and stood firm in my choices.

I started deciding what was best for me without anyone else's input. After defining these things for myself, I drew some hard lines for those I loved. The boundaries I set in place were for *me* so I could be the healthiest version of myself.

My first big change was to quit fixing, enabling, and over functioning.

And I quit giving David waffles when he didn't want them.

Acquiescing

While waffling is indecisiveness—a failure to make up or change one's mind—Merriam-Webster defines acquiescing as such: "to accept, comply, or submit tacitly or passively."[4]

When I comply, either tacitly or passively, to someone else's ideas without considering my own values first, it breaks down my own solidity. I'd know what I *should* do, but I'd give in or acquiesce.

People pleasing is one example. Attempting to make everyone happy supplied the approval and acceptance I longed for.

---

4. "acquiesce." Merriam-Webster.com. 2011, accessed May 4, 2022,
   https://www.merriam-webster.com/dictionary/acquiescing.

I knew there was a truer version of me—I'd seen her in my professional life. The place where I consistently stood firm was my real estate business. It wasn't until I was able to identify that and compare it to how I ran my personal life that I noticed an issue.

I arbitrarily thought about how I might respond to unusual requests of a homeowner while at a listing appointment. If a client wanted me to acquiesce to their ideas of selling their home and said to me, "You've got the listing, but I'll need you to clean the house, maintain the yard, and watch my kids from time to time," would I waver just to get the listing? Would I need to prove to them that I was a good real estate agent by agreeing to their conditions? No way!

In that scenario, I'd confidently say, "I do one job, and I do it extraordinarily well. I'll be your advocate and get your home sold because I'm excellent at what I do, but you'll need to find other professionals, like a housecleaning service, a gardener, and a babysitter, for the rest. I've got the marketing, selling, and closing of your home covered. Trust me; I know what I'm doing."

In my personal life, I was blown about by the wind with those I loved. I needed to get "the listing agreement" of those close to me so much so that I'd comply and appear unreliable. David couldn't depend on me to stand by him if I was trying to make it right for everyone—especially when those people were wrong.

Why did I acquiesce in my personal life so readily? Those I love have a bigger impact on me, and there's more at stake with the ones close to me—I can lose them. I developed anxiety, and in the past, I'd do whatever I could to lower that risk of loss. If I wasn't accepted, I felt unloved. And when I felt unloved, I felt alone. The deeper issue was abandonment.

We weren't meant to live life alone, but we also weren't meant to manage our fears by placing a Band-Aid over our traumas. I needed to approach my personal relationships the way I did as a solidified businesswoman.

I was too close to the situations of my personal relationships to clearly see. In business, I was objective because my transactions, while at times emotional for my clients, weren't emotional for me. Acquiescing was another way to avoid my own much-needed transition.

So, I took a new stance. Rather than give in to my worry by making everyone else okay (which would temporarily alleviate my unease), I faced myself. As much as I emotionally needed to quiet my anxiety through waffling and acquiescing, I also needed to overcome it.

I started paying attention to the instances of people pleasing that led me to waver in my beliefs. I began putting myself on the spot.

I forced myself to become uncomfortable in the face of anger and still hold my ground.

I no longer let myself take everyone's side and instead took the side *I* believed to be true. I gave myself the space to hold my own beliefs close without trying to change or conform to someone else's.

I peeked and spoke to my own issues, and it allowed me to see the worst of me yet *receive* the best of me.

I found the truest version of myself, and I felt confident in a whole new way. I was being true to who I really was, and in confronting myself, I began to stand firm.

Standing Firm

I started living differently.

With a wide stance, I planted my feet firmly on the ground and imagined growing roots deep into the earth. I would no longer be moved.

Standing firm begins by looking. You can't change what you

won't see. It's difficult to look at yourself with an honest eye, but I began with a quick glance.

When I started peeking, the real issue wasn't clear. I just knew I felt incongruent in certain situations. It took the help of my therapist to get deeper meanings. Once I understood, I had a choice to make: continue in the same cycles or step out and start anew.

After I saw the issues and chose to do something about them, I asked myself questions.

If I change this, how will that alter me as a person?

At the end of the day, who do I really want to be?

I acknowledged that there would be setbacks.

How will I handle the times I backslide or completely mess this up?

Who will challenge my new changes, and what will I do to overcome?

Then I put myself into situations where I could practice combating my waffling and acquiescing. With time and practice, I became immovable.

Learning these principles helped me receive and *not* receive, but what did that actually mean?

There are things that we're supposed to receive: compliments, gifts, goodness. But I'm also called to receive things about myself that I don't want to look at because they're too hard to face. God calls me to work on these to reach attainment.

There are also things I'm not supposed to receive because if I did, I'd need to learn to release them, like falsely accepting my childhood giants or wrongly taking on fears that drove unproductive behaviors and arguments. Yes, there certainly were things I needed to release, and I'd discover more of them as I progressed in my journey.

In applying the lessons I'd learned thus far, I freed myself up to open my heart to a truer version of me to God and others.

I was more readily looking within and being truthful with myself, and I was beginning to accept what God revealed about my own heart. I opened up and honestly evaluated what others said and weighed their opinions on the scale of *objective* truth, deciding whether or not to receive.

I asked myself tough questions like, "Is this true about me?"

In certain circumstances, I said, "Yes, I can see that. Perhaps I need to work on that to better myself."

And I got to the point where I confronted claims that weren't true.

"Do you consider me controlling because I question those whom I feel are lying to me?"

I could make an audacious statement like that one without emotion because I saw for the first time in my life who I truly was. *I* knew when I was being controlling and when I wasn't. I was able to respond to untruths without becoming offended.

In taking ownership of myself, I was open to receive the best and worst in me.

I stood strong in my own beliefs, decisions, and actions, and I transformed into a firmly rooted woman. I began really loving who I was *finally* becoming.

In a healthy way, I maintained my ground and believed in myself without changing my mind. If I did, it was because I was humble enough to receive a truth and reject the untruths, and I made solid decisions for myself without acquiescing to someone else's wishes.

To begin standing firm, we must start by peeking at ourselves. What's hidden in the dark must come to light, and the light can then change it.

God is light. He will illuminate our way.

Then, we open our hearts to a truer version of the self by learning the principles of receiving—knowing what to accept and what to release.

And it begins with a simple peek.

4

When Everything Stops Working

*You must be fearless enough to give yourself
the love that you didn't receive.*
—Oprah Winfrey

EVERYTHING DOESN'T AUTOMATICALLY STOP WORKING AT THE point of emotional fracture. Sometimes, things stop working long before we actually hit the bottom, but we choose to ignore the signs. Perhaps we're not ready to deal with areas that aren't operating well in our lives. Maybe we don't want to deal with our baggage, or we don't know how; we don't know what we don't know.

In my own life, in my desert decade, while I was striving to keep everything financially and emotionally afloat, I didn't know any better. I couldn't see that my efforts to keep me and David close weren't working. In hindsight, things never really worked as they should have, and we both needed to address our childhood giants way before 2017.

After discovering how far apart David and I had drifted in the beginning of 2018, the storm pressed on as I neared my emotional breaking point. I took my first step up the mountain and sought the consistent help of a therapist. I faced my own disappointment, the death of a dear friend, and extreme challenges in my own family.

My heart had withered from insecurity, failures, holding on to control, people pleasing, enabling, etc.

I realized I had a choice: either stay at the base of the mountain in the dark shadows or climb to find the light. The journey seemed too hefty, and a deep depression surged at the thought of so much wasted time. I didn't want to let one more minute elude me. If I was going to do this, I had to discover the best of me and get the most out of what future time I had left.

When it feels like all is lost, resilience of the human spirit can still be found. I needed to find myself again—or perhaps for the first time. I decided to pull from what faint strength I believed was within, ascend, and discover my deeper truths.

Deeper Truths

I was six years old when my family was at a horse race. My older cousin, Sammy, asked me to take a walk with him. I didn't want to, but I couldn't decipher why. Reluctantly, I left the safety of my parents to wander off into the crowd. We weaved through a sea of people. The deluge of bodies surging forward to wager made me feel woozy.

When I turned to ask my cousin to take me back to my parents, he was gone. Panic rose from my stomach to my chest, and I heard the little girl inside me scream, *Alone, alone, I'm alone! What do I do?*

I looked to my left and my right but recognized no one. There was a set of stairs before me where everyone headed to place bets, so I took my first step toward them and saw my grandpa walk past the bottom. I cried out, "Grandpa!" Tears welled as I called to him again, but he didn't hear me. My little feet chased after him, but by the time I reached the bottom, he was nowhere to be found.

I sobbed as thoughts raced through my young mind. *I love my family. I want to go home with them. But now I can't find them. Who will care for me? What did I do wrong? I knew I shouldn't have left. I'll take the blame. Just please help me find my mom!* Paralyzed in my fear, I started imagining the person who'd take me home to *hopefully* care for me.

Then a woman knelt down next to me. "Where are your parents, honey?" she asked.

I could barely get the words out as I said, "My cousin left me…I can't find them…My grandpa was here…He's gone."

She took my hand and started leading me somewhere, but Sammy and my mom appeared then, and I exhaled at the sight of them.

This memory and insight revealed where my fear of abandonment originated. And it created a childhood giant that followed me into adulthood.

Because I'd been working closely with my therapist, I started recognizing false narratives that lived on the inside and discovered the strength to face them. As deeper layers were uncovered, I opened to learning from them and became honest with myself. Ultimately, I took those insights to God for His direction so He could teach me what to receive and what not to.

In hindsight, my fear of abandonment kept me from receiving what I needed during our financial crises. It had deep subconscious roots that wouldn't let me objectively look at what was truly happening to me during my wilderness/desert decade.

While living through the economic downturn, I pushed through without truly giving myself grace and space to see that I was struggling. I wouldn't accept what was actually happening because I was scared to death that David would never be the same. I lived in fear that we wouldn't make it emotionally and was afraid to see what I was truly made of.

Therefore, I pressed on without listening to my soul or my husband's pleas and simply followed my own mantra—I can do it.

But it left me feeling very alone with thoughts that I'd be abandoned. What I didn't realize at that time was that this fear ran deeper than I comprehended. Subconsciously, I didn't want to be that little girl who was lost at the racetrack, frozen and scared. All of that caused disconnect in our relationship, and I lost who I truly was.

That hidden fear I hadn't pinpointed yet eventually resurfaced, but by that time, I'd found a healthier way to face the deeper workings within—seek them out rather than let them catch you off guard.

God didn't want me to just push through either; He wanted me to grow. And in order to grow through a situation, I had to face the facts: I was afraid of being left alone. That was the deeper truth to my pretense. Knowing that and with God's loving help, I eventually overcame the anxiety of abandonment.

Discovering New Pathways

Many of us share this deep longing for connection and the fear being alone. When Adam and Eve disobeyed God in the Garden of Eden, separation occurred. Adam and Eve doubted God because Satan deceived them. In that deception, they dismissed there'd be consequences for not taking God at His word when he said, "You are free to eat from any tree in the garden; but you must not eat from the tree of the knowledge of good and evil, for when you eat from it you will certainly die" (Genesis 2:16-17 [NIV]).

This was physical death as well as an emotional cutoff from God.

When they ate the forbidden fruit, they were kicked out of the Garden of Eden and out of God's presence, which began humanity's fear—separation from our Creator. It wasn't until God came to

Earth in the form of a man named Jesus who lived a sinless life that we actually saw His physical presence once again. After Jesus died on the cross to restore our reunion with God, God sent His Holy Spirit to be with us and live within. Now that we have the Holy Spirit, we're never truly alone, even if sometimes it feels that way.

We live in a fallen world where we're still susceptible to fears, especially abandonment and separation. So, we look to flawed human relationships to fill the void that can't be filled by anyone or anything except for God. He's the only one who brings ultimate peace and draws us into His loving presence. Until we're restored to perfection and dwell in God's presence again, it may feel like we need this constant reassurance.

The fear of being alone runs in my family. When my mom was growing up, her mother, Neva, had a blood pressure issue and would pass out from time to time. As a little girl, my mom was beyond frightened when that happened, and it left deep anxiety within her of being left alone. While this was extremely traumatic for her to experience at such a young age, we all have a choice: to either keep the family fears alive and pass them down to future generations or overcome them.

I decided to tackle my fear of abandonment by doing Eye Movement Desensitization and Reprocessing (EMDR) therapy. EMDR is an integrative psychotherapy approach that's been extensively researched and proven effective for the treatment of trauma.[5]

My definition of EMDR is that when we sleep, we dream, and dreaming is the way the brain processes the events of the day. When

---

5. "Experiencing EMDR Therapy," EMDRIA, accessed January 25, 2022, https://www. emdria.org/page/120.

a person suffers a trauma, many times they're not able to sleep and can't completely process what they've experienced.

EMDR uses sound (via earbuds) and light to make the eyes move, which recreates rapid eye movement that happens when dreaming. As you visualize an event in your life, coupled with the sound and light of EMDR, you process it the way you would if you were dreaming and then can heal from that trauma in your waking life. It allows the brain to make a new pathway so recovery and healing can take place.

I was skeptical as I sat across from the therapist. She asked me to think back to the horse racing track. As I did, I watched the events of that day play out as tears streamed down my cheeks. When I shared the memory with her, she asked me to go back to that moment and picture Jesus there.

Sound and light filled my senses as I freed my mind to create a new version of the racetrack narrative without consciously thinking about it. My brain freely rewrote the scene without any conscious input. It felt like watching my own internal movie.

I saw my young self at the top of the stairs, standing alone and frightened. Except that time, I spotted Jesus at the bottom. Relief washed over me as I ran toward Him. He swept me up in His arms and asked, "Sweet girl, why are you afraid?"

I responded, "I'm afraid that I'll be left alone. And if I'm alone, there will be no one to love me."

He smiled sweetly. "But I'm here. I'm always with you. And I love you like no one can. I love you with an everlasting love that'll never leave you. No one and no circumstance can take that away from you."

My small arms wrapped around His neck, and I felt safe, like an older brother had rescued me. Jesus gently placed me back on my feet and took me by the hand. He led me to my grandma, who swept me up and said, "Oh, D, I sure do love you. You'll never be alone. I'm always here to care for you."

That new version of the day's events created a new pathway in my brain and brought tears of joy and relief to my eyes. I felt my heart rate slow and a peace wash over me.

Once the EMDR therapy sound and light stopped, I removed my earbuds and returned to reality, wanting to tell my therapist about my new narrative. "No matter what circumstance I find myself in, I can call on Jesus. He's always with me, waiting to take me to a safe place. He will never leave me or forsake me."

She nodded her head as if to say, "Yes," and I knew it was an affirmative amen. I left therapy that day with a new outlook: I'm never alone, and when I feel lonely, all I have to do is look to Jesus.

After EMDR therapy, I was able to see Jesus at the "bottom of the stairs" of all my problems. I faced my fears and started praying differently.

"Jesus, I'm feeling lonely. Can we talk about this? I invite You and Your healing power into my space of fear. Jesus, I need you to replace my fear with Your peace. I accept all that you have for me right now, and I know that together, we can overcome this. Help me to remember my childhood racetrack experience the new way you revealed to me. Help me to always remember that You are with me. In Your holy name, I pray."

Until all is made new and right in the world, God is with us, even when we can't see Him.

Can you visualize Jesus at the bottom of your stairs? Or wherever you need Him to be so that you understand you're not alone?

Here's where to begin, preferably *before* everything stops working.

Receive the soul-stirring moments, however they come, and let them move you to awareness, searching deeper within. Be watchful of recurring themes.

For me, it was a returning feeling that what I was doing in my desert decade wasn't working. I felt unsettled and scared, but I didn't understand why. I needed to dig a little deeper to discover what was incongruent within before I could face it. Now, I understand that my efforts were to avoid being alone. Even if what I was doing wasn't working, it was better than the alternative, or so I thought. I know that's an untruth now.

Rewrite the narrative. If you don't have access to EMDR therapy, recreate the memory in a new and improved version. Allow the scene to play out in an altered and healthy way and let that be your new narrative.

In Matthew 18:3 (NIV), Jesus spoke these words: "And he said: 'Truly I tell you, unless you change and become like little children, you will never enter the kingdom of heaven.'"

Before Jesus made this statement, His disciples were arguing about who among them would be the greatest. So, Jesus put it in perspective for them. He told them they have to become like children. We must understand that in Jewish culture at that time, children had no say or power. So what Jesus was teaching His disciples was that they needed to be humble and dependent upon God to provide for them—like little children—if they wanted to please God and have the correct mindset to enter heaven.

We can't possibly make these mind changes solo; we need God's wisdom to help us shift perspective. So, we invite Him into our stories. We take our childhood experiences and how we remember them and give ourselves the freedom to create and think with child-like faith in order to rewrite the scene for a better story.

In my new version of the racetrack story, I allowed myself to think like a child. I was then able to conclude the memory with Jesus holding my right hand and my grandma holding my left as they walked me home. I even had a protector walk in front of us—Aslan, the lion from the movie *The Chronicles of Narnia*. My recreation was a healthy narrative that brought peace and a new way of conquering my fears.

By digging to discover deeper truths, we're loving ourselves in the deepest way. These discoveries make us fearless and capable of, as Oprah Winfrey said, "Giving yourself the love that you didn't receive."

And once you can love yourself, you can then open to receiving. But you first need to understand what it is.

I think the idea of receiving is like catching a ball. If you refuse to catch the ball, the game ends pretty quickly. We have to catch it in order to participate. Perhaps someone is throwing you some good advice—offering help or an opportunity—in which case, it's good to receive.

We also have to throw the ball back; we give so others can receive.

However, you get to decide whether you want to play or not. There are times we catch things we don't want, like childhood giants, negativity, or untruths. In those instances, we don't want to receive.

You can welcome in good things while also blocking out the unhealthy.

By continually acquainting yourself with your deeper truths, you begin to identify what's fit for you and what's not. In time, it becomes more natural to open your heart because you're capable of accepting and rejecting.

Everything that comes to us is not equal. My ten-year wilderness season might be insignificant to what you faced, or my journey might seem daunting. Regardless how painful the plight, to become our true selves, we must learn what and how to receive and what not to. We have one question we must ask ourselves: "Do I accept that, or do I or reject that?" And once we know how to answer honestly, only then can we become free to receive.

One of the things that helped me learn this principle was tactical training.

Awkwardly Training

I've always been the uncoordinated kid.

In school, classmates always chose me last for any type of sports-related activity, and being picked second-to-last was a good day. I was awkward in doing anything that took coordination.

Because I wasn't gifted in athletics, I shied away from that kind of activity. It just wasn't enjoyable and was sometimes painful.

Ten years ago, my friend, Kimberly, talked to me about tactical training and learning about firearms. All I could do was laugh.

"That's funny." I snorted.

"I'm serious. We live in unpredictable times, and you should learn how to protect yourself—especially working in real estate."

I thought about my unskillful self utilizing a firearm, and I began to laugh uncontrollably.

I was hardly understandable through my hysteria. "I'd be lucky if I shot the ground."

Now tears of laughter were manifesting, and Kimberly couldn't help but join me.

I barely got the words out. "I didn't know you could injure dirt!"

We continued until our sides hurt. As our silliness subsided, I simply said, "How about if you just protect me?"

"Happy to, but I can't be with you every moment. This is something you need to learn for yourself. You should be able to take care of *you*."

I left that coffee date actually considering the idea. I don't even know why other than the fact that it simply intrigued me. Could I actually learn this despite my limitations?

Months later, I took my first introduction class. I was frightened by the idea of handling a firearm, but by the end of the day, Kimberly helped me turn that fear into a healthy respect for what I was doing, and I actually did well and felt pretty accomplished.

I took more classes, trained at a range, and made some new shooting buddies who helped me improve. One of them invited me to a place in Nevada for a four-day handgun course.

I distinctly remember sitting in the classroom and listening to the instructor tell us something that's never left me.

"You have to decide first if you're capable of defending your life. In other words, in a life-threatening situation, could you pull the trigger?"

I blinked at the question. While I said to myself, *Yes, if my life was in danger, I could pull the trigger*, how does one truly know what they're capable of? Honestly, I wasn't certain.

The instructor's next words lingered the most. "You have to determine what you're willing to do in any given situation *before you're ever in a situation*. You have to decide this: who am I potentially willing to go to jail or die for? Carrying a firearm is an immense responsibility, so you have to figure out what you'll do and think about different situations that you might need to perform in."

It was overwhelming, yet impactful.

That night, I sat on the hotel bed and processed everything I'd learned and practiced over the last three days, all while taking note of how I felt.

Empowered.

I began to believe that I could defend myself and learned the power of the mindset, not knowing I'd eventually crave that new way of thinking and train more.

Sitting there that night, I didn't know that my new skills would become part of my regular practice and that I'd sharpen my abilities with my new shooting buddies more often. I experimented with different holster positions, learned how to respond to various situations, and understood a new way of thinking.

By training, I became at ease with who I was and how I responded to life's targets rushing toward me. I discovered that I didn't have to accept my uncoordinated self or allow it to hinder me. With some practice, patience, and mentorship, I emerged focused and capable.

I also understood that I didn't have to take on the deeper untruths that hindered me; I could, with God by my side, rewrite old narratives into new ones—ones that built up and reinforced my truest self.

Now, I wouldn't wait until everything stopped working to make my first counter move. I'd take the offense and write new narratives that reminded me I was never alone, I had the strength to overcome, and I was the one who needed to give myself the love that I craved.

Yes, I set my sights on something bigger. By realizing that, I got to decide how I would respond in any given situation. My tactical training not only helped me believe in myself, but it taught me the principle of what to receive and what to reject.

Sitting in the run-down Nevada hotel room that night—before my last day of class where I was due to take a final exam after a long, exhaustive day of training—I felt renewed.

Something had changed on the inside. I had no idea that the training would pay off in such a huge way.

In fact, it saved my life.

5

Pulling the Trigger

*Everything comes to us that belongs to us
if we create the capacity to receive it.*
—Rabindranath Tagore

IT WAS JUST ANOTHER PREDICTABLE DAY HOLDING AN OPEN HOUSE —
or so I thought.

Turning on all the lights and arranging the brochures on the kitchen bar, I'd only been there five to ten minutes tops when a loud knock turned my attention to the door. I tucked my phone into my front left pocket and proceeded to the entrance.

A tall man with a tattoo on his neck stared back at me. He stepped in as I introduced myself and walked into the townhouse toward the living room. I diverged into the kitchen, and we began a conversation with a breakfast bar between us that separated the kitchen from the living room.

The man asked how long the place had been on the market while he took a brochure and looked at it. I asked him where he lived.

"I'm just a couple of blocks from here. I have two roommates, and I'm not sure two bedrooms would work for the three of us. How large is the second bedroom?"

"It might fit two small beds, but I agree that it'd be a bit small for the three of you."

"Will you show me?"

He walked back toward the front door, and I exited the kitchen before we both merged at the bottom of the stairs.

He was uncomfortably close.

In my unease, I took the first step, and as soon as I did, I knew I'd placed myself in a position of weakness.

A millisecond conversation took place in my head.

Dawna, you never let a stranger stand behind you. Now there's no exit except going past him.

I owned my action of taking that first step. I'd committed to walking in front of him; so, as we ascended the stairs, I turned sideways to watch him. He spoke first.

"What do you know about VA loans?"

"Have you served in our military?"

"Yes, I *was* a Marine," he replied.

A deep unease swept through my stomach. Quickly, my logic reminded me the past tense "was" isn't used with Marines—once a Marine, always a Marine, unless they're no longer alive. But this guy was still breathing and following me up the stairs.

He's not a Marine.

Halfway up, I looked him in the eyes and said, "Thank you for serving our country."

"Oh, sure," he said, but he didn't catch my gaze. In fact, he refused to look at me. His casual and calm response scared me even more.

My gut instinct grew stronger. *Something's not right.*

I quickly searched my mind as we approached the top of the stairs, needing to find a way to create space between us. The only way to get some distance was to go into the master bedroom and position myself on the other side of the bed.

He blocked the door and the only way out, and suddenly, it all went down.

He lifted up his shirt, pulled out a twelve-inch knife, and slammed it down on the bed.

"This is a knife, and this is bear spray. Take off your ring and get in the closet. Now!"

At first, my mind played catch-up with what was happening. It felt like I was thinking so slowly. *Why is he pulling up his shirt? A knife?*

But when he said the words, "Take off," the action of him drawing something from his belt—the bear spray—kicked in my tactical training.

As he untethered the bear spray from his waist, I reached for the firearm in my holster. When he saw it, his eyes opened wide as a gasp escaped him, and he sprayed me at the same time I pulled the trigger. The spray hit me as the bullet went past his shoulder, and he ran down the stairs. After taking a quick breath, I followed him and kept my mind focused on the incredulous moment. I stayed close enough to know where he was going, but the bear spray blurred my vision. My skin started to burn, and it was getting harder to breathe. As I reached the bottom of the stairs, he ran out the front door.

Coughing to clear my lungs, I got to the kitchen sink to rinse out my eyes with the cool water. Once the burn soothed, I could see enough to call 911.

I slid my hand to my front pocket and was surprised to find my phone still there.

Ring, ring...

As I waited for the operator to answer, logic was still somehow present. During my training, I learned to identify the necessary: name, location, and problem. My ability to do that under extreme stress startled me.

"Nine-one-one. What's your emergency?"

I stated the important points so the operator knew the facts and to send help quickly.

"My name is…

"I'm located at…

"I've been attacked by a man at an open house.

"I have a conceal carry permit, and I have a loaded firearm on the kitchen counter.

"I need police and an ambulance.

"I'm going to go lock the door because I can't see very well, and I don't know if he's coming back or if there are others.

"I need you to confirm when the police arrive."

And then I broke down, shaking uncontrollably.

"What do I do? Everything burns, and I can't see!"

"Keep rinsing your eyes. The police are on the way."

"Will I lose my eyesight? What if I pass out and the police can't get in?"

As soon as I'd stop rinsing, the pain worsened. *What's happened?*

The fog from the bear spray permeated the whole house, and it continued to get more difficult to breathe.

Finally, a loud knock came at the door.

"Commerce City Police. Open the door."

"I need you to confirm this is really the police," I told the operator on the phone.

Hesitantly, I walked over toward the front entrance.

"Hold on a minute. I'm confirming."

Through the slats of the blinds and the blur of my vision, it seemed like there were people in uniform.

"Dawna, I've confirmed that it is the police. You can open the door."

Two male police officers rushed in and immediately started coughing and gagging as a woman pulled me out to the front porch.

Paramedics tended to me as the female said something. My head swirled at the rush of adrenaline.

"My face, arms, and chest burn. I can't see very well."

The woman spoke again, and I turned my attention to her.

"My name is Dory. I'm a CSI agent."

Through the haze, I squinted at her.

"I've been sprayed with pepper spray, tear gas, and bear spray before, so I know how you feel. Here's the deal: the next twenty-four hours are going to be painful, but you need to deal with it! Get your mind right, and focus."

I turned inward, dug deep, and received her words. I focused on the coming relief of the next day as I centered my mind, and the police department called David.

"'This is the police department; we're with your wife. She's been attacked but is okay."

Click. The phone call dropped. Three times.

David had given up on the details. He'd put a T-shirt on inside out, got inside his truck, and headed north. He wasn't sure where he was going, so he called my best friend, Julieann, whom I call Buddy.

On the hour-long drive, Buddy researched the closest hospital to the open house location while talking to David to keep him calm.

Dory looked at me just before the paramedics closed the ambulance door, and the reality of my situation made me erupt into tears.

Her tone softened until it was sweet and calm.

"You did the right thing," she said.

My response surprised us both.

"I know! I saved my own life! But I just fired at another human being. He was wrong, but still, I need to process what just happened."

Tears rolled down my cheeks and made my eyes burn even more. I realized crying only exasperated the issue, so I held back my full emotions.

Her silhouette backed away from me and out of the ambulance.

The paramedics closed the doors and continued flushing my eyes and rinsing my skin. The ride to the hospital took forever, so my mind drifted.

I needed David. I sincerely hoped he was on the way.

At the hospital, they gave me some medicine to help counteract the reaction of the bear spray. Apparently, it was oil based, so it'd take some time to remove. When they applied water, I felt temporary relief before the extreme burning returned.

David walked into the room and looked perplexed as his eyes fell on me. My skin was bright red like a tomato. He'd finally heard what happened while being escorted to my room.

He held back tears. "Did he touch you?"

"No, thank God! I'm okay."

He sat beside me and tried to look brave.

"I fired at another human being."

He took my hand gently. "Good."

I wanted him to hug me, but my upper body was too sore. "When can we go home?"

There are things that push you over life's edge and events that cause you to either free fall into despair or make you more rooted within.

After my decade of trials, especially in the last year, I would've guessed that those agonizing circumstances would've ripped me from the soil and left me withered; instead, it forced a new strength within me I never thought or realized I had.

In the face of danger, I took care of myself and did what I was trained to do without any hesitation. Before the attack, a small part of me wondered if I could actually protect myself.

During the training, I was asked, "In a life-threatening situation, can you defend yourself?"

I'd answered, "Yes," but no one can be sure until faced with a real-life situation.

I learned to receive all that had transpired in the last ten years, but I had to allow it to transform me for the better.

That night, David helped me into the house and walked me over to the couch. It'd been a long day, and my skin felt like someone was holding a blowtorch up to my face and upper body.

Wearily, I sat down. David had to run a quick errand, and a moment of panic rushed through me.

Don't leave me, I thought.

But I knew he had to go.

"I'll be back in forty-five minutes tops. You have your phone, so just call me if you need anything."

I blinked but said nothing. If someone were to break in while he was gone, I wouldn't have been capable of pulling the trigger again. I felt hazy.

My mind searched for a plan, but things were still foggy. So, I just sat with my trauma, unable to decide whether I could get myself to the kitchen for some water.

The fan David placed in front of me to keep the burning at tolerable levels blew at a steady pace. All I could do was recall the events of the day as objectively as possible.

I did do good.

I thought about how I received the signals that things weren't right and adjusted my plan as they played out. I remembered how quickly I had grabbed my firearm, even though it felt like it happened in slow motion. I had known my life was in danger, and that was what I'd trained for.

I didn't hesitate. I pulled the trigger and saved my own life.

My mind wandered to when I took that first step at the bottom of the stairs. I didn't beat myself up about that decision and gave myself grace on how well I handled everything else.

Suddenly, an image flashed through my mind of Jesus at the bottom of the townhouse stairs. He didn't stop the incident from happening, but I knew He was protecting me somehow.

He was with me. I wasn't alone.

Pulling the trigger meant finding the strength to care for myself in the face of trials and letting God protect me. The way we perceive life's circumstances is key; we can either be open to them or closed.

Rabindranath Tagore said, "Everything comes to us that belongs to us if we create the capacity to receive it."

I believe there's a little more to this quote, so here's my version:

God will allow circumstances to come to us—some we need to embrace and some we don't. The key is learning the difference between the two and finding the wisdom within to receive and reject.

While "hits or misses" can be the difference between life and death when firing at unwanted circumstances, most importantly, we can't freeze. We must be able to pull the trigger.

Part Two

How to Choose Well

6

Confronting Yourself

Holding onto yourself requires giving up
your favorite ways to dodge self-confrontation.
—David Schnarch, PhD

CHOOSING WELL AND KNOWING WHAT TO ACCEPT AND WHAT TO reject is vital in our efforts to become the truest version of ourselves.

We stop evading ourselves and refuse to live with the childhood giants that bind us. Instead of feeling like we're locked inside, we unbar the hindrances that keep us from being free and begin to see someone deeper and more solidified—we hold on tight to our inner strength.

The open house attack could've been a point of emotional fracture.

"That's it! I'm done."

"Really, God? You allowed *this* too?"

"What did I do wrong to deserve this?"

Do these statements resonate with you? At times, I've uttered very similar words, except the open house gave way for my inner strength to rise to the occasion.

Has she always been there? And why, for so many years, was she so hesitant to reveal herself?

I started confronting myself—a self-double-dog dare.

My recovery from the incident could've gone one of two ways. I could've interrogated myself by saying, *Dawna, you're so stupid! How could you make the mistake of going up those stairs first?*

Or I could decipher what I could've done differently in a healthier way.

In the days that followed, my thoughts drifted to dark places. The attack could've turned so grave. He could've knocked me out going up the stairs, or my firearm could've snagged on my holster and not come out quickly enough, or he could've jumped over the bed and stabbed me, or worse. I needed to get my mind right fast.

I thought about how I would've handled and responded to different scenarios, then I faced and loved myself.

Confronting myself looked something like this: *Okay, for whatever reason, you took the first step and allowed a stranger to walk behind you—not a wise decision. How would you respond now knowing what you do?*

I paused to think and put my answers in my journal, allowing time to take an honest look at the situation from every angle. After evaluating, I said to myself, "Yep, I'll own my decision. If I'm in a situation like that again, I won't go up the stairs first. Heck, I might not even answer the door."

I acknowledged my newfound wisdom and said, "I'm wiser now. I won't do that again."

I gave myself grace and space. Grace says I can't be "on" all the time—one can't make correct choices every waking moment. That day, I wasn't on my best "yellow alert." Yet, I tend to beat myself up and spend too much time trying to be perfect.

Looking at myself objectively like a fly on the wall, I examined what I could've done more skillfully, but more importantly, what I did right. There were a lot of things I did well, so I congratulated myself. I held the open house incident in my mind, flipped it around, and looked at it anew.

I listened to my intuition when I went up the stairs. I made space in the master bedroom and was decisive in the face of danger; I took action when my life was threatened.

My healing from the attack had begun.

That's why confronting yourself is so important. It forces you to examine the true inner workings. Sometimes, those places are difficult to look at, but you begin to see that perhaps you've lied to yourself. And while those lies serve a purpose, like lowering anxiety, they don't allow you to face the true you.

Or maybe you don't believe in yourself—falsely thinking that you aren't capable of making sound decisions or of deciphering what's right. If you discover that you spend too much time waffling and wavering, it might be time to resist and try a new approach.

We don't find our truest selves in comfy spaces, so we challenge ourselves by moving into uncomfortable situations.

Confronting yourself can also reveal some beautiful insights too. You begin to release being "on" and perfect all the time, and you start to see the good things within and the right choices you made by appreciating and loving yourself more. A confident feeling of knowing that you've got this takes shape, so you can move to a more purposeful place.

The day after the open house attack, I went to the police station to give my testimony. After two hours of sharing and recalling the incident to the best of my ability, I was asked to do an interview with various news stations.

I was mentally exhausted from reliving the day, let alone dealing with the remnant effects of the bear spray that still lingered on my skin. So, I didn't feel up to doing the news interview, especially after being given a pre-news interview pep talk by my victim's advocate.

"Remember, don't talk when the media comes in because they're always recording. Be careful with your words so they're not twisted into untruths. And there are many people who don't like guns, so be mindful of what you say about them. I'll be here if you need assistance during the interview."

I looked at David. "Tell me *why* I should do this."

He took my hand. "Because it's the right thing to do. It might help catch this guy."

My knight in shining armor, David, encouraged me to stand up to my fears. He gently reminded me to do what was right even though I was anxious about the interviews.

I took a deep breath as the media came in.

The interviews aired that afternoon. Many of my friends, family, and clients saw different versions of the news stories on TV and social media. Text messages, phone calls, and PMs of well wishes poured in, and I was overwhelmed and grateful for all the love and support.

The next day, I received a call from the police department.

"We need you to come down to the station again; we believe we have the suspect."

I sat in a small dark room with an officer who held out a handful of mugshots to me.

"I want you to look through these and tell me if any of them look like the one who attacked you."

I closed my eyes. *God, give me clarity. Help me know for certain if one of these images is my attacker.*

I took the photos in my hands and looked at the face on the top of the pile.

Nope.

I placed it at the back of the stack and looked at the next one. *Nope.*

My gut tightened at the third picture, though. His eyes looked right at me and took my mind back to where it all happened. It was him.

I looked at the last two images, but neither were familiar. I was left holding my perpetrator's mugshot, and although it didn't show his neck tattoo, it was definitely him.

I pushed the headshot toward the police officer. "This is him."

"Are you certain?" he asked.

"Yes."

My perpetrator was booked and taken to jail.

Later on, I found out that it was because of my news interview that the police were able to find my attacker, and they recounted the story to me.

●●●

There was a construction worker working two blocks away from where my open house was held. He'd found a can of bear spray and threw it into his truck bed. When he got home, he gave it to his wife, who apparently was also a real estate agent. He told her he'd found it in Commerce City while working and wanted her to keep it in case she ever needed to defend herself when showing property.

She told him about the news report she'd seen on TV, and they called the police. The can of bear spray he found was the very one that was used on me!

My perpetrator had also left the knife at the scene, and the officers were able to match his fingerprints to the brochure I'd handed him at the open house. With all the evidence—and his previous criminal history—they arrested him.

After many court hearings, the man took a plea agreement and was sentenced to jail for fifteen years!

I realize many stories don't always have happy endings that lead to arrests or closure, so I'm fortunate mine did. And all because I was able to confront myself, recall the situation, and look at it from different angles. I acknowledged what I could've done better and what I did well. I allowed myself to be proud that I committed to my decision to pull the trigger in order to defend my own life, and I knew I did everything to the best of my ability. I pressed myself to do the news interview that had no guarantees of a positive outcome and received all of myself with loving correction and affirmation.

Some asked me if I shot my perpetrator.

As I pulled my firearm out of the holster, I aimed it at the threat. When the blast of bear spray hit me, I squeezed the trigger, and the bullet whizzed past his shoulder and landed in the drywall just behind him. I didn't take another shot as he ran away because I was in a townhouse complex with common walls where bullets could penetrate and he was fleeing.

Aim well in life. Many times, you will hit your target. Sometimes you'll miss, but you don't always have to strike it. In my case, I legitimately pulled the trigger, yet missing still worked in my favor. A miss means you didn't freeze and you took action, which is a score.

What creates a steadfast man or woman of God is being able to take decisive action. Standing firm is about owning your decisions—not waffling or wavering, holding up the results of your actions and looking at them honestly without beating yourself up, and saying with conviction, "I did a great job."

There'll always be times where you feel you could've done something more skillfully, but as you train in being the person you want to be, you'll grow into someone stronger than you ever imagined.

The open house attack aided in a newfound resolute me. I had the courage to face my adversary, and I tapped into a deeper strength I didn't know resided within me.

Soon enough, it was time to confront the other areas of my life: the *unhealthy* within me. It'd take courage to hold on to myself and not let go of the good within.

Confronting myself was the first step to facing my giants—only then could I slay them. I pulled the trigger in my own life and made healthy decisions. Facing my own self was the first step in learning to completely receive.

And I chose well.

7

Becoming Ready

Be ready to catch the ball
when it is thrown by life.
—Steve Jobs

SOMETIMES, WE'RE SIMPLY NOT READY, PREPARED, OR PERHAPS even equipped to receive. Life plays out in rugged terrain, and experience opens and closes our hearts. In order to avoid shutting down altogether, we must be clear about what's vital to us.

Even today, I'm still learning about my own clarity. In many circumstances, I can't articulate what's bothering me. At times, I'm uncertain as to what I need to make myself feel protected and secure.

During my desert decade, I just wanted everything to be right again. I thought I knew what was important—changing our financial outcome in the midst of a recession and helping David regain his confidence. But my situation clouded my viewpoint, and I didn't see what I needed to do for *myself.*

I didn't know how to confront myself and face the childhood giants I was unaware of. I'd never learned to articulate what was important to me.

What I knew to be true at the time was that David and I needed financial provision because the economy became graver by the day.

As David struggled, I spent my time trying to fix our situation, coveting my old comfy life.

While I thought I'd defined my needs—make money and help David—vagueness was my companion. I asked questions about external problems and ignored the internal. *How can I make money to sustain us? In what ways can I help David?*

Tackling those two complex issues was definitely necessary, but I'd neglected myself.

At the beginning of our financial collapse, I became focused and driven. I revamped my business plan and grew my career in a declining market. I was leading financially and sustaining us at the same time.

As the market slowly shifted upward in 2012, David and I began doing fix-and-flips—buying homes at auction, fixing them up, and reselling them. Things seemed to be getting better.

But I still needed clarity about my own struggles instead of fixing everyone else's. I was afraid to look at my own weariness, and I couldn't quite define my boundaries. I needed to learn what it meant to receive, reject, and apply these principles in my life, but I didn't know how.

The way I became ready was through my own circumstances. And many times, that's the way it has to happen. Hitting rock bottom either keeps us flat on our face or forces us to do something about our situation, but I want you to know that it doesn't have to. You can prepare to be your best self before you think about needing to be ready. Then, you can catch the ball when life throws it at you and have the wisdom to know if you even want to catch it.

Think of receiving like playing basketball. Sometimes you have the ball, you dribble, and you're strategic in making your next shot—you're basically in control of your own game. You've received self-control, goodness, patience, and faithfulness, and you can calculate what's best in any given situation. You're open to compliments, grace, acceptance, rest, kindness, gentleness, healthy competition, and desire, and everything seems to be "in your court."

There will be times when the ball is taken from you. Still, you're prudent, able to evaluate when to regain control of the ball, and wise enough to know *if* you even want it at that point. You understand there are situations where you catch the ball and should hold on to it as well as times you need to let go.

When life chucks a ball at you, you have the wherewithal to capture it or to step aside and dodge it altogether. The art of receiving means you know and understand when to reject the things that aren't good for you. Whether you see it coming or are totally caught off guard, healthy non-receiving is just as important to play your best tournament.

Becoming ready to receive has to start by evaluating your own game.

Who are you? What do you need? How can you play your best by being true to you in every way and being proud of who you've become?

In 2018, I started training in my own life game. I learned how to understand my inner workings, and I discovered that I was dissatisfied with certain parts of me. I didn't like that I'd taken so long to draw lines with others and that, at times, I didn't stand up for David the way I should've. I didn't like the girl without a courageous voice.

I needed to receive honesty with myself, gracefully acknowledging that I could've done things more skillfully. That didn't mean I'd carry the blame; rather, I'd own up to my part and gently receive. I knew I needed to take a hard look at my core values.

Reflecting on the past, it would've been helpful to address my own loneliness and weariness and face the fact that David and I had grown distant. If I'd gotten the help I needed when I needed it, I would've been more in control of my own destiny and been able to listen to my instincts. I would've believed in myself more and articulated clearly and precisely.

Now, when a situation or something that's said doesn't sit right with me and I just don't know why, I inquire within.

What's bothering me about this? What did he say that made me feel uncomfortable?

Sooner or later, leaning into my deeper ongoings will become clear as long as I keep searching. Eventually, I'll get clarity. *Yeah, that's why.* Or, *Oh, that's it.*

Once we're willing to truly confront ourselves and clarify our needs and what's important, then we can understand what to accept and reject. This is how we prepare to open our hearts to receiving.

I challenged myself and made huge changes in my life that set tough boundaries with those I loved. I even removed some unhealthy family relationships, and I began accepting the fact that I did everything I possibly could, with the tools I had at the time, to lead our family and help David get back on his feet.

I began to see how I'd evaded myself by filling my void with other things such as women's ministry. *Doing, doing, doing* kept me from seeing. It kept me busy and deflected from asking defining questions that forced me to look at reality.

I wonder how things would've turned out if I'd had the ability to ask myself and others questions clarifying my own needs. Things like:

I feel like I've given you all that I have, yet you still seem distant. What's going on with us?

I need help carrying this load.

Why I am pouring myself into others—meeting with so many women to help them—when I'm exhausted myself?

I feel lonely.

Do I need counseling?

What if I'd asked myself deeper questions and listened to my weary soul? Would we have taken a different path instead of traveling down a broken road?

Receiving must begin with a clear, internal understanding of yourself and caring for your heart's desires. I'm not referring to acting on every feeling to make yourself happy; I'm talking about the needs of your soul for tender loving care. Those are spaces where only God and you, together, make yourself better and ready yourself to face anything.

Becoming ready to receive begins by deciphering those longings, confronting yourself, taking inventory of what you need to be healthy, and addressing it long before daunting circumstances hit. In doing so, your heart readies itself to open up to healthy events and close up to unproductive things in life. This'll crack the door of your heart and invite in what's good for you.

May we learn to be prepared in advance of difficult life situations so we can receive and not receive—knowing what's best for our hearts. Confront yourself and take steps to become ready. Receive what's good. Reject what's not.

Open your heart, friend. You can care for it best. It'll be okay. Choose well.

8

Receive Not!

The giant in front of you is never bigger
than the God who lives in you.
—Christine Caine

I WAS LEARNING HOW TO EMOTIONALLY CARE FOR MYSELF. Realizing more each day that I'm only responsible for my own inner well-being, I started to discover contentment. I understood that I had the power to control my emotions, and I repeated to myself, "No one can make you happy but you."

But my whole world was still David. So, I became intent on adapting a healthier version by grasping the concept that I can be okay even when he's not. We were emotionally fused, and I needed to learn how to detach myself in certain instances. This gave me the strength to work on myself and the grace to stop fixing everything for everyone else. I found that being present, listening, and helping *when asked* actually brought deeper connection.

One thing I had to learn not to receive in my life was doing too much to my own detriment. I can't be all, do all, and fix all, especially when it hardens my heart. When I feel irritation, discontentment, or bitterness, it's time for me to re-evaluate what I'm doing and change direction. If I don't, it'll lead to resentment, and that's not healthy for relationships.

When David was struggling, it wasn't up to me to make everything in his world right again. I could've asked if he needed help, but it wasn't healthy to jump in and start patching and mending. Perhaps David needed to find his own way.

I had to figure out a new way of interacting with my husband, but as a recovering "fixer," it was beyond difficult.

David was working full time on his new career as a day trader trading the stock market. When he'd have a tough day, the old me wanted to run to his rescue and help, even though I knew nothing about trading stocks. I felt my anxiety ramping up in his struggle; not only did I want to fix his day, I wanted to shush my unease within. I'd soon discover this wasn't healthy for David, me, or our relationship.

Nowadays, working *on* and not *over* functioning, I simply walked alongside David. Rather than encouraging him, I gave no answers or solutions. I sat next to him and looked at his trading monitors as he showed me graphs and charts and explained why a trade should've worked. I shook my head in agreement, listened, and quieted myself in the midst of an internal tornado that worked to uproot my inner calm.

I said things like, "Based on your data, I see where you would've thought this trade would work."

"I believe in you."

"You were meant to do this."

"I'm sorry you're having a tough day; how can I help?"

"You must be so discouraged."

"What can I do for you in this moment?"

I said all that while dealing with my own fears inside my head.

Fix it quick. If David's not doing well, we as a couple aren't doing well. What if he disconnects again? DO SOMETHING, ALREADY!

I learned about the power of overcoming fearful feelings and practiced self-control. Besides, that was his new career, and he needed to figure it out without my interference. I'd give my opinion only when he asked me to.

It was exceedingly difficult for me to do nothing in the midst of David's struggles. But with little input, I was able to receive his journey and simply be his sounding board, which drew us closer and helped me let go.

There were moments when he had a tough day, and I couldn't be there for him. On those days, I felt overwhelmed and unable to pour into him, but it was good and healthy as I deciphered what I needed too.

In those moments, listening weighed me down. It drained me, and I needed to be full before I could give to him. When I noticed what was happening, I knew it wasn't good for me to hear him out. So, I'd simply say, "Today, I'm feeling overwhelmed with your discouragement, and I need to step away for a while." David was gracious and understood that I needed to care for myself in those circumstances.

We shared highs and lows and were blessed with days when his trading was prosperous and he felt encouraged, so we learned to navigate both the winning and losing days. Loving David through his struggles and stepping away actually opened a new dimension of intimacy—that's our huge win.

While our deep knowledge of each other developed by sharing our lives together over thirty-five years, that loving act of living alongside him without fixing, enabling, or over functioning made our connection deeper than we'd ever experienced. It was beautiful and one more layer of something only the two of us shared.

I started saying, lovingly and firmly, in various relationships, "David, I love you, but I can't help you with that right now," or,

"Mom, I'm sure you'll make the best decision with whatever you decide," and, "No, I can't meet this month. How's your schedule for next month on this day?"

I no longer ran around like an idiot trying to fix everyone's problems. I drew strength from letting go and taking care of my own needs—I opened my heart to myself.

Still, there were instances where I'd slip back into my old habits, so I attempted to define what it meant to accept or reject in my life.

I leaned in to receive and receive not.

Not receiving—closing the heart to things that aren't healthy for you—looks like this:

- Letting go of the outcomes you want when it depends on someone else. Remember, you can only change you.

- Refusing to engage in something that breaks your values.

- Blocking and ridding yourself of gluttony—the habitual greed of wanting excess.

- Cleansing the heart of revenge, hate, fear, envy, idolatry, and coveting.

- Understanding the difference between desire and lust.

- Closing up to pride and opening up to humility.

- Learning to control what you can and releasing what you can't.

- Rejecting untruths that someone is trying to tell you when you know they're false.

- Declining unsound advice.

- Doing something for someone else that makes you feel resentment, anger, or discredits who you are.

- Not only keeping out the giants that create feelings of inadequacies or failures but actually slaying them.

What else can you think of that you need to receive *not*?

In what ways do you need to accept or reject those things that come your way?

One way I decided to block the things I shouldn't take into my heart was to slay the giants that taunted me.

Slaying Giants

I stared at the stone I'd picked up from the brook in the Valley of Elah, the actual place where King David knelt to select his own five smooth stones before encountering and fighting Goliath.

The stone I brought home from Israel seems to speak from ancient days. Perhaps it's an eroded but better version of its larger self from thousands of years ago. Maybe it represents the worn-down me who's evaluating her life and making it more beautiful.

But before that famous moment came to be, David fought other battles to prepare him for his moment in the Valley of Elah. In 1 Samuel 16, God instructs the prophet Samuel to travel to Bethlehem and anoint one of Jesse's sons to replace Saul as king. Jesse had eight sons but only brought seven to Samuel. Each passed by, and Samuel said to Jesse, "The Lord has not chosen these. Are these all the sons you have?"

Turns out there was one more—the youngest who was tending sheep, David (1 Samuel 16:1-13[NIV]).

I read the story and inserted myself there. How did David handle this childhood trauma of not being chosen by his own father? He wasn't even considered until Samuel asked if there were any other sons. And still, David showed up, stood before Samuel, and received the anointing of oil. Only then did the Spirit of the Lord come upon him.

The scripture says that God looked at the hearts of Jesse's sons, but He saw something profound in David's. What was it? Could it be David's ability to receive and not receive?

Receiving the anointing without arguing or questioning—simply with an open heart? Not receiving the thought that he was chosen last, nor buying into a false belief that he wasn't first?

Having an open heart and knowing when to close it invites bravery that's needed to look honestly and deeply within—something God asks us to do throughout our lifetime. I had to look closer at how young King David did this.

Receive Your Anointing

I went back to the scripture and imagined young David in the fields shepherding. He seemed oblivious to Samuel's search for the next king of Israel. He wasn't looking to be chosen; he simply looked after his father's sheep. He didn't need more. He'd received his calling way before Samuel anointed him with oil. The moment David's father put him in charge of tending and protecting the herd, David was already fulfilling his calling. It's what he loved to do. Shepherding in the fields was God's preparation for David's future position—protecting and shepherding the Israelites as warrior and king.

So, when David was called to be anointed as future king, he simply stood there and received. He wasn't looking for more, but if God asked more of him, David would've obliged.

As I looked at young King David's life, I wondered what other things God might call me to if I wasn't searching for more or asking for roadmaps. What would it look like if I was content and not chasing after extra attendees for our yearly conference, additional women to help, or more readers?

What would happen if I became satisfied with the position He'd given me? How would I feel if I stopped looking for more and embraced the sheep He's called me to protect and defend? Could I allow myself to live in the unknown—that which God already knows?

We need to receive what God gives us because He knows what's best. It all starts with openly receiving without our own agendas. Just like young King David, each of us has a specific calling in our lives; all we have to do is follow his example.

When David was called to shepherd, he did so. When he needed to protect, he fought. When called by his father to meet Samuel, he went. He accepted Samuel's anointing without knowing the way to kingship. All he was told was that the Lord had chosen him, and David accepted.

By accepting his calling, being content with what God put in front of him, and trusting, he became a man after God's own heart. He was then capable of looking into his own life and into situations without hesitation. Perhaps his ability to truly see himself began when he received the anointing from Samuel and God—opening his heart to "peeking" at things he'd later discover about himself and changing for the better.

At that moment, he had no idea that he'd springboard from the shepherd boy who protected sheep by killing lions and bears to slaying a huge giant and saving Israel. Preparedness comes when we, like David, contently accept our calling and trust God along the way.

If you want to slay your giants, the first step is to receive your anointing. Like young King David, you'd willingly say, "Yes!" to your royal calling. Allow the anointing oil to pour over your head and cover you to your toes, then step into your greatness.

If you stand on the shoulders of your giants, you'll see farther, but you'll never be able to slay them with a single stone unless God is by your side. And you must slay them in order to claim your royal position.

Question and Declare

After David's anointing, he served King Saul. In between serving King Saul and tending to the sheep, David's father sent him to bring food to his brothers, who were serving in King Saul's army at war with the Philistines. When David approached the battle lines, he heard the giant Philistine, Goliath, threaten the Israelites. David questioned, "Who is this uncircumcised Philistine that he should defy the armies of the living God?" (1 Samuel 17:26 [NIV]). The inquiry also made a declaration: *I don't care how tall he is; he's no match for God.*

David asked about God's opponents, but never the sovereignty of God. By asking that, he not only placed doubt about the authority of Goliath but forced the Israelites to look into their own hearts and see their fear for Goliath. He also made a declaration—a profound statement of faith—that *no one defies God,* and they'd lose if they did.

* * *

In contrast, when I felt God leading me to combat my fear and write my first book, I told Him, "Lord, you've got the wrong girl. I have a science degree; I'm not an English major. Certainly, there's someone more qualified."

Writing was an unknown giant at the time. If I'd only responded like young King David and said something like, "Who is this unwritten book that she would defile my heart with fear and doubt the living God?" I eventually wrote, but not without arguing.

King David asked other questions that made profound declarations. After his statement about the uncircumcised Philistine, Saul sent for David, who said, "Let no one lose heart on account of this Philistine; your servant will go in and fight him" (I Samuel 17:32 [NIV]). Saul told David he couldn't because he was just a boy and the Philistine was an experienced warrior. But David, in not so many words, asked Saul an important question. He said, "Why do you believe it is *I* that will fight Goliath?"

David proclaimed to Saul, "More so than Goliath, I've been training with God for this moment in time my whole life. When I tended sheep for my father, I fought off lions and bears. How is Goliath any different?"

He convinced Saul to let him fight Goliath in his final declaration, "This uncircumcised Philistine will be like one of them because he's defiled the armies of the living God. The Lord who delivered me from the paw of the lion and the paw of the bear will deliver me from the hand of this Philistine" (I Samuel 17:31–37 [NIV]).

I pondered the depths of this young man's words. How many times in my decade of trials did I think the fight was up to me? How often had I let fear keep me from fighting my giants and forgotten it's God who wins the battle?

We need to question the Goliaths in our lives and confront the Sauls and every circumstance that comes against us. We should question our hearts and fears and identify everything that's against God's will while making statements of declaration that become affirmations because we're anointed. God is with us and for us. He will lead the way and fight for us.

Run

The famous Jonathan Cahn—Rabbi, author, and speaker—was the head tour guide during our trip in Israel. He staged a reenactment of the David and Goliath scene, and the story came to life as we watched the battle between boy and giant.

As I stood with the tour group in the Valley of Elah, Rabbi Cahn split our group of three hundred in half. I looked at those opposite me who were playing the part of the Philistines. A very tall man was instructed to be Goliath.

Standing in front of my group was Rabbi Cahn's son playing the part of young King David. Each group shouted at one another—a Bible scene portrayed right before my eyes.

Then "Goliath" recited his lines. "Am I a dog that you come to beat me with a stick? Come here, and I will feed your flesh to the birds of the air and the wild animals of the fields" (I Samuel 17:43–44 [The Voice]).

The young boy responded, "You come to me carrying a sword and spear and javelin as *your weapons*, but I come armed with the name of the Eternal One, the Commander of *heavenly* armies, the True God of the armies of Israel, the One you have insulted. This very day, the Eternal One will give you into my hands. I will strike you down and cut off your head, and I will feed the birds of the air and the wild animals of the fields with the flesh of your Philistine warriors. Then all the land will know the True God is with Israel, and all of those gathered here will know that the Eternal One does not save by sword and spear. The battle is the Eternal One's, and He will give you into our hands" (I Samuel 17:43–47 [The Voice]).

Then, the young boy ran toward Goliath. Rabbi Cahn interrupted the reenactment and ruffled his son's hair. The boy asked,

"Dad, did I do good? I didn't disappoint you, did I?"

Rabbi Cahn responded with a chuckle and said, "You did well, son." Then he continued with his message. "David ran toward his opponent. This is how we need to combat the fear and opposition in our own lives—running forward with the faith of victory in our hearts."

I stood there deep in thought as our two groups merged back into one and headed to the same brook where David knelt to collect his five smooth stones before fighting Goliath. As I stood there watching, feelings rushed back from the last two years of my life. Did I respond in the ways King David had in the face of adversary? Had I received the anointing of my marriage and truly believed that God brought my husband to me and me to him? In the dark winter of 2017, had I questioned the enemy and declared God's purpose and victory in my marriage? Did I fight by *running toward* my fears and conquering them?

Standing in the Valley of Elah while everyone gathered stones in the brook, hope filled my heart. Even though it felt like I was as frozen as the frightened Israelites when faced with fear, I actually did face my giant.

I'd received and believed that God brought David and I together because that night in his uncertainty, I said to David with conviction, "Despite your own confusion right now, I still love you. I've always loved you and have been in love with you and only you." Remembering the strength of my own words brought tears to my eyes.

I also questioned and declared. I remembered entering 2018 with a warrior heart as I placed anointing oil over the doors of my home and spoke words of battle. "Don't lose heart. Don't be afraid. Who is this uncircumcised darkness that defiles the marriage of God?"

And I ran toward my adversary and landed in the arms of God. I walked around my house and created an invisible prayer circle of protection around it and around me and David. I received God's promises about the protection of my marriage; looking back, I'm amazed at how steadfast I was as I stood in the face of adversity.

Even though I was scared to death, I faced myself and became brave enough to peek. I started with looking first at my own emotional dependence and sought out help for it. I stood firm in my faith and claimed reconciliation in my marriage—working hard on what *I* could change in *me*. Somehow, I knew I faced a giant—perhaps the biggest one I might ever fight.

I walked to the brook, which had become a dried-up riverbed. I knelt and quietly gave thanks, picking out a stone that now sits on my desk. This eroded but better version of its larger self once sat in that same brook thousands of years ago. It's broken, but it's beautiful. The edges had been smoothed from caressing living water, similar to God smoothing out the edges of my own life—it was a difficult, but freeing, process.

Perhaps King David's battle with Goliath was just the precursor in learning to fight greater giants—his own future giants within.

I, too, had to receive my anointing, question and declare, and then willfully choose to run toward (and not away from) my inner giants to slay them.

There's power in self-mastery.

Christine Caine said, "The giant in front of you is never bigger than the God who lives in you."

Once we accept our anointing, we're fully equipped with God's power through His Spirit, and we have everything we need to conquer our giants.

Jesus received His anointing when He was baptized in the Jordan

River. King David received his from Samuel when he stood under the anointing oil.

We then declare God's word and question the enemy's; in this case, the enemy of our soul is Satan. The Bible tells us in 1 Peter 5:8 (CJB), "Your enemy, the Adversary, stalks about like a roaring lion looking for someone to devour."

So, we question the enemy like Jesus did when He was tempted in the wilderness in Matthew 4:1–11 (NIV):

> Then Jesus was led by the Spirit into the wilderness to be tempted by the devil. After fasting forty days and forty nights, he was hungry. The tempter came to him and said, "If you are the Son of God, tell these stones to become bread." Jesus answered, "It is written: 'Man shall not live on bread alone, but on every word that comes from the mouth of God.'" Then the devil took him to the holy city and had him stand on the highest point of the temple. "If you are the Son of God," he said, "throw yourself down. For it is written: 'He will command his angels concerning you, and they will lift you up in their hands, so that you will not strike your foot against a stone.'" Jesus answered him, "It is also written: 'Do not put the Lord your God to the test.'" Again, the devil took him to a very high mountain and showed him all the kingdoms of the world and their splendor. "All this I will give you," he said, "if you will bow down and worship me." Jesus said to him, "Away from me, Satan! For it is written: 'Worship the Lord your God, and serve him only.'" Then the devil left him, and angels came and attended him.

Satan uses our inner giants to keep us from the full promises of God. He attempts to keep us feeling trapped within, but we have God's Spirit, His power, and His words in the Bible to overcome and slay our giants to move into freedom.

"For the word of God is alive and active. Sharper than any double-edged sword, it penetrates even to dividing soul and spirit, joints and marrow; it judges the thoughts and attitudes of the heart" (Hebrews 4:12 [NIV]).

Jesus questioned Satan and declared God's word. David questioned Goliath and proclaimed God's victory. Both King David and Jesus ran toward the adversary and slayed him.

Do you realize you are called for a specific purpose? Have you accepted your anointing?

Where are you this very moment? Running away or running toward your giants?

What needs to die within so that new life can spring forth? In other words, what is the biggest thing in your life you need to reject? And might you invite God in so He can help?

Receive your anointing. Question all that comes against you. Declare God's word over your life. Then run toward and destroy your giants.

It's good for us to know what to reject in our lives, and slaying giants is one of the many ways to receive *not*.

9

The Ultimate Receive

Therefore I tell you, whatever you ask for in prayer,
believe that you have received it, and it will be yours.
—Mark 11:24 (NIV)

I WAS STANDING IN FRONT OF A PILE OF RUBBLE, NOT REALIZING that something profound was about to transpire.

I'd just come from the top of Mount Moriah where the Dome of the Rock resides—a sacred site for Muslims, Jews, and Christians. The Dome of the Rock was built over the holy rock where Muslims believe Mohamed ascended to heaven. For Jews and Christians, it's believed that the rock was where Abraham took Isaac to be sacrificed and where the first and second Jewish temple resided until the destruction of the second temple in 70 AD.[6]

After visiting the Dome of the Rock and Temple Mount, our tour guide, Maya, led us down the side of Mount Moriah to the City of David. I gazed at the excavated stones from thousands of years ago, which are the remains of the ancient walls of King David's home.

Maya shared with us. "My father is an Orthodox Jew. I'm not sure if he would be pleased with me telling this story because tradition teaches that while in the City of David, nothing bad shall be said about King David."

----

6. "The Destruction of the Second Temple," Jewish History, accessed January 25, 2022, https://www.jewishhistory.org/the-destruction-of-the-second-temple/.

Sweet Maya paused to look at us. She gave a tight-lipped smile, which was something she did unconsciously as a signal to pause and reflect on her words.

I knew what was coming next: the story of King David and Bathsheba. Staring at the old walls of King David's kingdom, I imagined him standing on his rooftop and looking at the beautiful woman bathing herself.

Maya resumed. "And while I'm not sure if my father would like me telling this story, I believe it has a significant message we need to know." She read 2 Samuel 11:1–26 (NIV) from her Bible.

"In the spring, at the time when kings go off to war, David sent Joab out with the king's men and the whole Israelite army. They destroyed the Ammonites and besieged Rabbah. But David remained in Jerusalem. One evening David got up from his bed and walked around on the roof of the palace. From the roof he saw a woman bathing. The woman was very beautiful, and David sent someone to find out about her. The man said, 'She is Bathsheba, the daughter of Eliam and the wife of Uriah the Hittite.'

"Then David sent messengers to get her. She came to him, and he slept with her. (Now she was purifying herself from her monthly uncleanness.) Then she went back home.

"The woman conceived and sent word to David, saying, 'I am pregnant.'"

Maya closed her eyes, summarizing the rest from memory.

"David decided to fix the situation quickly. He ordered Bathsheba's husband, Uriah, to return home from battle. Uriah stood before King David while he said, 'Take a break, go home, and be with your wife.' But Uriah didn't go. He respected King David too much, so Uriah slept at the entrance to the palace with all his master's servants and didn't go down to his house. The next morning, when questioned by King David, Uriah said, 'My commander Joab and my lord's men are camped in the open country. How could I go to my house to eat, drink, and make love to my wife?' Since Bathsheba's pregnancy couldn't be covered up in the way King David had initially planned, he conspired to have Uriah killed while in battle."

Maya looked down at the stone floor with sadness. She reopened her Bible and read from 2 Samuel 12:1-10 (NIV).

"After King David's orders were carried out to murder Uriah by placing him in danger on the frontline of battle, the Lord sent His prophet, Nathan, to tell King David a story. It was about a rich man who had plenty of sheep yet stole a poor man's only lamb to give to a traveler.

"When King David heard the story, he burned with anger and said to the prophet Nathan, 'This man must die!' Nathan replied, 'You are this man! The Lord says, "I gave you everything, and if this was too little, I would've given you even more." Why did you despise the word of the Lord by doing what was evil in His eyes?' David immediately received Nathan's rebuke, admitted to his sin, and received forgiveness from the Lord."

Maya paused and smiled again before continuing. "I'm in the City of David, and I'm supposed to follow the tradition by speaking only good things about King David—the man after God's own heart. But this story of great failure is for all of us. We can mess up big time and still be anointed by God. When we're open to receive from God—especially when He tells us to repent or says, 'Don't go that way,' or 'I have better plans for you than that'—we need to open our hearts to Him and simply receive. If we don't, we might never know what our unique calling is capable of and may never fulfill the true promises of God in our lives."

I was swirling. How many times had I not received from God—

brushing off His rebuke or rejecting His warnings? Where might I be today if I'd learned to openly receive from God? While standing in front of the remains of King David's home, something wouldn't let me be—one line from that scripture…

"In the spring, at the time when kings go off to war, David sent Joab out with the king's men and the whole Israelite army. They destroyed the Ammonites and besieged Rabbah. But David remained in Jerusalem" (2 Samuel 11:1 [NIV]).

Why did this one statement linger with me? *But David remained in Jerusalem.* I was flooded with questions.

Why wasn't King David doing his lifework—fighting with his men on the battlefield? Was he restless because he wasn't fulfilling his purpose as a warrior? Had God intended him to be in battle, yet he chose to stay home? And if he'd gone, would the whole trajectory of his life have turned out differently? Would adultery and murder have never taken place?

As I asked myself those questions, I understood that we're not able to simplify human behavior to "If that transpired, then this would have happened," or "If I didn't do that, I wouldn't be here." That's black-and-white thinking, and life plays out in the gray.

The human heart longs to make sense out of things and explain the equations of our lives. We want to pencil out A plus B equals C. My heart cried out, "Oh, King David, if only you'd followed God, then those grievous sins never would've happened."

But our decisions don't follow simple linear equations. Perhaps life's choices are like complex math problems—not all solutions come from one way of solving. You can get to the right answer through different computations, and an incorrect answer can come from miscalculation, poor choices, or enemy interference. Correct calculations always have God in the solution.

We're complex beings with free will, so God allows us to choose and struggle and permits the enemy of our souls to interfere.

Sure, I can theorize that if King David went into battle instead of remaining in Jerusalem, it would've thwarted his actions of adultery and murder. But would it have thwarted exposing his heart? And isn't a pure heart the ultimate answer?

Regardless if King David stayed or went, God worked on something much bigger—exposing the human heart for what was hidden inside. God used David's grievous decisions and the situation to create pure motivations, and David received.

Standing in front of the remains of King David's house, my judgment of his actions dissipated. With my heart convicted of my own grievous sins, I opened my hands to receive from God in that very moment. I whispered from within, *God, what's hidden in my heart that you want me to see?*

Silence.

As Maya continued talking about archaeology and findings in the area, I asked again.

God, what's hidden in my heart that you want me to see?

A faint and familiar voice whispered back. *Resentment lingers in the corners of your heart.*

I recited in my mind the heartfelt cry from Psalm 139:1 (NIV): "You have searched me, Lord, and you know me."

I knew exactly what God was asking me to do—let go of the past.

I held some resentment toward God and others in my life. I'd worked hard to become the woman I wanted to be—someone steadfast, loving, and hardworking—but God allowed my tough journey to transpire, one of financial loss, stolen identity, and ultimately, distance from the one I loved. *How could He let that happen?*

I felt like I gave my all—not perfectly, but as best I could.

Yes, resentment lingered.

I needed to let go of resenting my husband and being mad at God for allowing the disconnect in our marriage. I needed to receive what God was doing *now* and respond with repentance and acceptance of what God would do moving forward.

I had to quit rehashing. "If only things would've gone differently, then that wouldn't have happened." And suddenly I found my hands and heart had opened. Like King David, I received His rebuke and His love as His peace found its way into my heart.

With that new enlightenment, my negative emotions from all I'd been through softened. The group stirred, ready to head to the next location. As Maya continued, Proverbs 31 came to mind. It described the ideal woman who lived a life of integrity, but something else was revealed.

It's believed that the author of Proverbs 31, named King Lemuel, was actually King Solomon—King David and Bathsheba's son.[7] It's also said that the Proverbs 31 woman was written by King Solomon about his mother. If that was true, how would that change my perceptions of "the ideal woman"?

The "Wife of Noble Character" brings her husband good all the days of her life. She is a hardworking businesswoman—an entrepreneur. She does philanthropy and cares for her household. She is strong, full of distinction, and doesn't live in fear. Proverbs 31:25–26 (CJB) says, "Clothed with strength and dignity, she can laugh at the days to come," and "When she opens her mouth, she speaks wisely; on her tongue is loving instruction." She could very well be Bathsheba—the one who sinned with King David.

Despite that, she became the woman she wanted to be. Even

---

7. "Who was King Lemuel in Proverbs 31?" Got Questions, accessed January 25, 2022, https://www.gotquestions.org/King-Lemuel.html.

though scripture doesn't mention her repentance like it does King David's, she also accepted God's rebuke and became the "ideal woman." She turned from her past and became all the things that scripture said she was:

- She brought good to her husband her whole life.

- She was a good businesswoman. (I believe she was a real estate agent because she "considers a field then buys it" [Proverbs 31:16 (CJB)].)

- She tended to the needy and the poor.

- She didn't live in fear.

- She was wise with only good things to say.

Bathsheba, despite her past, became an astounding woman while David became the man after God's own heart, and all because they both received and moved forward.

Our tour group headed on and exited the City of David. That day, I also walked forward into the future of what God had for me with my high school sweetheart, David. I metaphorically stepped out of resentment and into a new version of myself. Resentment still crept back into my heart from time to time, but I immediately noticed it and took it to God, allowing His shalom to replace it.

No matter what you've done, it's never too late. God will still use you. If God can restore King David and Bathsheba, He can do the same for you. All that's needed is to receive from Him.

What's keeping you from these high positions? What do you need to receive right now? Forgiveness? Direction? Faith?

Ultimately, God wants you to receive His love and the gift of salvation. It's time to receive from the Master so He can recalculate your next season.

It's as easy as opening your heart and receiving Jesus into your life.

Mark 11:24 (NIV) says, "Therefore I tell you, whatever you ask for in prayer, believe that you have received it, and it will be yours."

Receiving His salvation is more than a future in eternity with Him; it's also about harnessing His presence to live in the moment. So, be free to believe that you've asked for not only eternal salvation but also the ability to seize the rest of your moments with God's help and companionship.

Let the scripture bring to mind God's power that resides within, and may it remind you that by allowing your heart to be open to what God has for you—all of the trials and blessings—you're living out His direction for your life. Ultimately, it's what God wants for you. For all of us. He longs for us to receive Him in all aspects of our lives.

In those moments at Mount Moriah, my heart became excavated. Like the exposed rocks of King David's house, I felt as though I was discovering something new within. I longed to be more honest with myself, more open to receive from God, and more vulnerable with my husband.

I believe Maya's father would be proud of her for sharing the stories of King David's failures in the City of David. Maya didn't succumb to man-made traditions that persuade us into speaking or acting the way others think we should. He'd be pleased knowing that his daughter, through her honest and neutral storytelling, helped me think differently and discover the importance of receiving and the power that comes from truthfully sharing our experiences.

In the "City of Dawna," there's been a tradition I've maintained: hide my life's stories that don't make me look the best, especially the things I don't love about myself and the places where I've failed miserably. I pushed them deep down or shoved them aside, never to be looked at or talked about again. Except that approach injures the soul.

Instead, I've learned to identify those spaces I don't want to see, allowing God to come into those tender places and receiving Him. This is true especially if His rebuke has consequences, as King David's sin had.

In 2 Samuel 12:7–10 (NIV), God said to King David, "I anointed you King over Israel, and I delivered you from the hand of Saul. I gave your master's house to you…And if all this had been too little, I would have given you even more. Why did you despise the word of the Lord by doing what is evil in his eyes? You struck down Uriah the Hittite with the sword and took his wife to be your own. You killed him with the sword of the Ammonites. Now, therefore, the sword will never depart from your house, because you despised me and took the wife of Uriah the Hittite to be your own."

The ramification of their sin resulted in the death of David and Bathsheba's first-born son.

Sometimes, receiving our rebuke and consequences are heartbreaking. But King David faced God and received his with strength. And once he did, God healed the parts of his wounded soul that desperately needed more of Him.

Receiving the Father's rebuke in love is sometimes difficult, but it'll transform a life and heal a soul more effectively than anyone or anything. We must be honest *and* gentle with ourselves—allowing space and grace and loving ourselves as God does while working on His required change within us. We should mimic King David: be quick to receive *everything* from God.

David Schnarch, PhD puts it this way: "You can't correct an error in judgment unless you recognize your mistakes."[8] This is the way we learn to completely receive. Just like King David, we must have a heart to receive God's instruction, His rebuke, and then modify our behavior in response to his infinite love.

I worked on opening myself up to God's ultimate gift and receiving everything He had planned for me. All of it.

---

8. David Schnarch, *Passionate Marriage* (New York, NY: W.W. Norton & Company, 2009), 376.

Part Three

Putting it into Practice

10

Doing This Together

None of us, including me, ever do great things.
But we can all do small things, with great love,
and together we can do something wonderful.
—Mother Teresa

RATHER THAN THEORIES OR IDEAS, I REACHED A PLACE WHERE I needed to put into practice what I'd learned to remind myself what worked and what didn't, remember what was true and good for my heart and what wasn't, and outline and implement processes that kept me moving in the direction I wanted to go—forward.

I'd reached milestones in my journey, recognizing I'd spent too much of my life receiving the wrong things like childhood giants, MM, pretending, waffling, and wavering.

I learned to stand firm, become brave enough to peek, discover deeper truths, and face them. I found new ways to create healthy pathways in my brain for my thoughts, and I learned how to confront myself and slay my giants.

Little girl lost was found.

I'd been training in transformation. Just like my tactical training, I created muscle memory by utilizing practices through my counseling that helped me pave a way to wholeness. What were the specific applications I utilized in my daily life that gave me the strength to harness what to receive, what not to, and continually grow forward?

My list included practices that focused on my mind, heart, and soul.

What begins in the mind makes its way to the heart and affects the soul; when the soul is affected, whether for better or worse, it plays out on life's stage.

I listed two focus areas that shaped the mind: homing in on my intuition and dropping the weight of negative thoughts about myself. Since scripture is adamant about controlling thoughts, "Take captive every thought to make it obedient to Christ," my first two practices dealt with the way I thought and how to shape that (2 Corinthians 10:5 [NIV]).

Next, I moved to the heart and implemented three more practices that identified my heart's motivation, pinpointed my thoughts and feelings and recognized who was really in charge of them, and finally learned how and when to open and close the heart.

For my soul, I made a breathable list with room for modification and truly found acceptance and my way to wholeness.

The practices in the following pages will give you the control to glance back, glean, and ultimately look forward in awe and wonder.

As you join in, it's important to read the practices in order. You might discover that the first or second are already in place in your life and you're ready to implement practice three or four. Each builds on the one before it until you're free to receive. So, trek with me one chapter and practice at a time. While training my mind, heart, and soul, I finally became completely free to receive.

I began living my life at full capacity. Plus, I didn't want to look back with resentment or regret, so I knew I had a choice to make: either live in dark spaces or look beyond and choose to see the good ahead.

The Bible reminds us to keep moving in Ecclesiastes 9:11 [NIV]: "The race is not to the swift or the battle to the strong," but to the one who presses onward, holding fast to God, until we reach our goal.

To not idly move through life, but instead live purposefully and be able to proclaim, "Wow! That was an incredible ride. It had so many twists and turns and highs and lows. It had uncertainty and moments of intense joy and laughter. I'm glad I had the adventure."

What kind of life are you looking for? One that's secure and easily calculated? Or perhaps you long for an incalculable challenge that ultimately brings meaning and purpose. You just need to look at yourself and your circumstances differently to alter the mind, heart, and soul and to extrapolate everything possible from this incredible expedition we call the human experience.

My friend, Allen Arnold, says, "Here's what it all comes down to. What kind of life do you want—a safe, predictable one or a story filled with mystery that forces you to lean into God?"[9]

I always wanted a safe and predictable life until I was forced into a narrative filled with unforeseen sharp curves. I almost got stuck there within the pages of life's assaults—only seeing the danger of the steep mountainside. But I chose to lean into God, recognize that he's my guardrail, and willingly venture with Him. With these coming practices and by relying on God, I not only made it to the next chapter, but I also got there glad for the journey.

----

9. Allen Arnold, *The Story of With: A Better Way to Live, Love, & Create* (2016), 283.

Make the choice now to implement these practices so you can turn the page of your life. It's never too late to write your next thrilling chapter.

Let's make this journey—*together*.

11
Practice One – Intuition

Intuition is the journey from A to Z
without stopping at any other letter along the way.
It is knowing without knowing why.
—Gavin De Becker

L ET'S GO BACK TO THE OPEN HOUSE SCENARIO. I'D FINISHED TURN-ing on the lights and readying the house, so I stood in the kitchen, putting brochures out on display. A loud knock came at the door, and I felt, ever so slightly, a tightening in my stomach. The reaction was barely noticeable but enough for me to take a split-second pause and say to myself, *That's odd.* The aggressive knock on the front door had signaled to my body that something wasn't right.

Typically, people would gingerly crack the door open and say, "Hello?" or stand in the entryway and ask if it was okay to walk in. In all my years of hosting open houses, I've never heard a forceful knock on the door like the one that day. Instead of paying attention to what I felt, I silenced my intuition, walked to the front, and let a strange man inside. In doing so, I'd just ignored my first warning sign.

That said, my intuition signaled me, but when I went to the front door, I let my logic decide if it was safe to proceed or not. My first impression of the man was reasoned through my past experiences. He looked like a thug, but I thought, *Okay, I have male friends who look like thugs, but they're as gentle as teddy bears.* So, I introduced myself to him as he entered.

He walked into the living room, and I stepped into the kitchen so the half-wall that separated the kitchen and living room stood between us. In the safety of my distance, we had a short conversation about how long the house had been on the market. Nothing seemed out of the ordinary until he asked to see the upstairs. I walked through the kitchen as he walked from the living room, and we both landed at the base of the stairs at the same time. It felt awkward being so close to him, and before I knew it, I took the first step. I knew the minute I did I'd just put myself in a position of weakness.

It's not that I had any other signs at that point; it's just that I know from my safety training that you should never let someone stand behind you—don't give anyone your back. The position of strength is always letting the person go in front of you so you can keep your eyes on them and secure an escape route.

I've learned invaluable skills through tactical training, like how to safely and quickly draw a firearm, clear doors, defend myself in any given situation, and have the right mindset—knowing what I'd do in any given situation before ever being in it. Part of the mindset training was awareness and being on "yellow alert," a higher level of preparedness.

I'm specifically fascinated with mindset because it helps you think through given situations and decide the best route to take before being in a difficult position. It's important to make mental decisions beforehand because you can't be certain you'd be able to make the right choices in the face of adrenaline-filled danger. If you wait until you're in a sticky situation, you run the risk of hesitating or freezing up, and it could get you killed.

Tactical training prepared me for the worst while hoping for the best, and I prayed I'd never need to utilize it. However, I was fortunate enough to have the knowledge that saved my life.

I'll admit I wasn't on my best "yellow alert" at the open house. The day before, I'd returned from a yearly girl's trip with Buddy. I took my firearm with me on our trip, fully prepared to protect us while we—two women in a strange state—were on the road together. All went well, and when I returned to Colorado, I exhaled knowing we both got back safely. I was back to just caring for my own safety.

The next day was the Sunday of the open house, and I was still on exhale mode. While not an excuse, I simply didn't listen to my first warning—the aggressive knock that signaled my intuition.

As I headed up the stairs, I realized I wasn't in a position of strength. So, I walked with my body half turned toward the man to keep my eyes on him. He asked me about a VA loan, and I'd said, "Oh, you've served our country."

He answered, "Yes, I *was* a Marine."

Immediately, my gut reaction was more intense.

As I approached the top of the stairs, I said, "Thank you for serving our country."

He wouldn't look me in the eyes but said very casually, "Oh, sure."

I'd never heard such a nonchalant response from someone who served in any branch of the military. I typically heard responses like, "Yes ma'am," or "It's my duty," or "It's my honor." Stronger than all the previous intuition warnings, I received my third signal as my gut tightened even more.

We were at the top of the stairs, and I knew something wasn't right. My body signaled louder and louder, and I understood something felt off about the whole situation. But I didn't have a way to escape. I was at the top of the stairs as he stood a few steps below me. Retreating back to where we came from was the only exit, and he was blocking my way out.

I knew from training that my best and only option was to create space between us. So, I went into the master bedroom and got on the opposite side of the bed facing him, and in an instant, it all went down.

What if I'd listened to my intuition the first time? Perhaps I wouldn't have been in the situation at all. How would my day have gone if I decided to go to the front door, lock it, and call for help?

Defining Intuition

So, what exactly is intuition? It's the body's way of alerting you to danger or warning you when a situation or someone isn't right. It's important to take note when something feels "off," and there's no need to understand, hesitate, or question—intuition just knows.

If intuition waits to reason, it could be too late.

So, we must listen to what the body tells us through its powerful signals.

Where do we sense or experience this?

When speaking to men and women about safety, I'll ask the question, "Where in your body do you feel your intuition signaling you?"

Many men say they feel intuition on the back of their necks, in their chest, and sometimes on their arms when their hair stands up.

Women, like me, feel it in our stomachs and refer to it as a "knowing in the gut." A friend once said that GUT was an acronym for God Under There. Regardless of where you experience intuition, it's important to listen to its warning signs.

Everyone has a God-given design of intuition; someone who doesn't believe in God still has intuition and the ability to hone it. However, once a person yields to God and accepts Jesus as their savior into their heart and life, they're filled with the Holy Spirit.

I believe that when the Holy Spirit resides within, intuition is heightened. And while you can train to tune into your intuition without knowing God, ultimately, trusting the Holy Spirit within is more effective.

It's far better and more fruitful to listen and follow the Spirit's guidance than to do it solo. A skill is perishable, but God's presence is not.

There are times when we logically argue, override, and ignore our intuition. The Spirit will send signals, but we have the freedom to either listen or disregard Him.

There are many reasons why we don't heed the warnings when something isn't right. For example, we may not want to believe what's happening is truly happening. We might believe a person is only capable of their best and not their worst. Many times, we don't *want* to see because it'll alter our relationships or change the status quo of our lives. When the complete truth is so life altering, we allow logic to tell us *that can't be* when in fact it is. That response protects us from the fear of facing reality and the anxiety of change.

While there are various rationales for why we shut out our intuition, more important is how we honor our internal signal, listen closely, and take action despite our perceived dreaded outcomes. Gavin De Becker says, "It is knowing without knowing *why*."

When we learn to trust our intuition without needing to know why, we're empowered to care for our own physical safety and our emotional well-being.

Knowing that, how would you pay closer attention to your intuition?

The more I've learned about intuition, the more rooted the belief "always trust your intuition" is. It will come to your aid as a lifesaving signal, as a guide in a major decision, and even as a way to either save or walk away from a relationship, but it's there to help.

Three Ways to Trust Intuition

When learning to have faith in my intuitive signals, I discovered three areas to work on:

- Decipher when you first started dismissing your intuition.

- Know the difference between feelings and intuition.

- Redevelop it.

Let's look closer.

I stopped trusting my intuition when I was a young girl. After some reflection, I remember the exact day I began repressing it.

I was in my teens when I shut down my inner wisdom. I quit listening to my gut because honestly, what it revealed scared me. Before this, at a young age, I felt so in tune with my intuition because it always seemed spot-on.

Sometimes, it was an inner knowing that a decision was right and that it was safe to proceed. Other times, it was a feeling that something bad would happen. Like the time I felt sick to my stomach all day only to get a call that my cousin Sammy was injured in a football accident and was on life support. Or the time I felt the negative energy of a family member who eventually was diagnosed with breast cancer. But the final thing that made me shut down my intuition was the day a warning came about my beloved grandma Caston.

One morning, I decided to visit Caston before she headed out to her son's office picnic. She lived right around the corner from my childhood home, so it was only a short walk. As soon as I saw her, I felt uneasy. Somehow, I just knew she shouldn't go to the picnic, but I didn't say anything. I believed that if I didn't confess it to Caston, then it wouldn't be true.

When I returned home, my mom noticed my worried face and questioned me.

"Mom, I know this is going to sound crazy, but something bad is going to happen to Caston."

"Oh, honey, don't say that!" she said to me.

Later that afternoon, we received a call from my uncle informing us that Caston had fallen at the company picnic and broken two bones in her leg. I questioned my decision. *Was I supposed to warn her and tell her not to go? What if I warned her and then nothing happened?*

I wrestled with my thoughts until I came to a conclusion.

"No more," I said. "I won't listen to this inner instinct again. You're officially tuned out!" And that was the day I repressed my intuition.

Somehow in my naivety, I decided that if I ignored these warnings, dreadful things wouldn't happen. But I discovered that restraining intuition doesn't prevent something terrible from occurring.

In hindsight, the intuitive feelings might've been the Holy Spirit telling me to pray. Perhaps I was being called to be an intercessory prayer warrior.

I might've also asked Caston, "How are you feeling today?" to which she probably would've responded, "I feel fine."

I could've shared something along the lines of, "I have a sense that something is off with you today. Do you feel up for this picnic? I know that you get nervous in crowds, and if you don't want to push yourself today, you don't have to go."

She would've still gone, but then I could've prayed fervently over her and left it to God.

How about you? Can you remember a time that caused you to shut out your divine intuition? I invite you to sit with it for a while. Tell it that it's all right to come back and begin listening again. That's the first step to welcoming it back in.

Thirty years later, I began tactical training and rediscovered intuition and the importance of taking notice of my inner signals. I received it and, once again, invited it in.

Perhaps you've never identified your intuition until now. Great! Today's the day to start honing your inner guide.

Next, we have to understand the difference between our feelings and our intuition.

Feelings come and go. They're grandiose in the moment, but once heard and respected, they typically settle down. Being worried about something that *might* happen is different from being in a distressing situation.

For me, abandonment and perfectionism are feelings from past experiences that are fleeting. Severe anxiety can hang on longer and present as intuition, but it's distinctly different from pure instinct.

While feelings try to hold on as they come and go, intuition nags, amplifies, and won't let up. It's such an intuitive knowing that something isn't right that it scares us to logic our way out of it.

At the open house, the knock on the front door alerted my intuition. That slight tightening in my stomach was intensified as danger crept closer and wouldn't leave. It was the knowing feeling that something wasn't right.

If I would've been more alert to it, I could've addressed it immediately to discern if it was a feeling or my intuition. It only takes a millisecond to say, "I sense you signaling fear. I'm paying attention." Then pause. Decipher if a feeling is being triggered from a past experience or, instead, a deeper sense of recognizing that something isn't right; "knowing without knowing *why*." De Becker names it "the gift of fear."

Intuition is the body's way of seeking truth, and it won't stop until you listen to it and resolve what it's alerting you to. This *knowing* from deep within must be heard.

I rediscovered it through firearm training, but I only applied it there. Being wiser, I saw I needed to apply my intuition in every area of my life. Like in my marriage, for example—if something David said didn't feel right, I'd ask him to clarify what he meant. If that resolved the unsettledness, then the feeling faded. If, however, it lingered, then I must trust my intuition to know that something still wasn't right and pursue what that was.

In his book *The Gift of Fear,* De Becker uses a great example of trusting your intuition. Airline pilot Robert Thompson walked into a convenience store, and for some reason, he was suddenly afraid. He turned around and walked right back out. Later that day, he learned about a shooting that happened in the store after he'd left.

"I asked him what he saw that he reacted to. 'Nothing, it was just a gut feeling,' responded Thompson. [A pause.] 'Well, now that I think back, the guy at the counter looked at me with a very rapid glance, just jerked his head toward me for an instant, and I guess I'm used to the clerk sizing you up when you walk in, but he was intently looking at another customer, and that must have seemed odd to me. I must have seen that he was concerned.'

"Thompson continues. 'I noticed that the clerk was focused on a customer who was wearing a big heavy jacket, and of course, I now realize that it was very hot, so that's probably where the guy was hiding the shotgun. Only after I saw on the news what kind of car they were looking for did I remember that there were two men sitting in a station wagon in the parking lot with the engine running. Now it's all clear, but it didn't mean a thing to me at the time.'"[10]

What I love about this story is that Thompson honored his intuition. Nowhere did he second-guess his decision to leave. He left the convenient store and never looked back. He didn't spend the next few hours justifying to himself why. He didn't beat himself up by saying, "I should've bought those magazines I went in there for. What's wrong with me?" Nor did he obsess over the news waiting for affirmation that something bad had happened in the store. He simply went about his day, trusting in what he felt without needing confirmation. He avoided a deadly situation because he believed in himself. He *received* his intuition.

To open my heart and discover the true me, I must be open without judging myself or my intuition because it's a gift worth honoring. "With judgment comes the ability to disregard your intuition unless you can explain it logically, the eagerness to judge and convict your feelings rather than honor them. Can you imagine an animal reacting to the gift of fear the way some people do, with annoyance and disdain instead of attention? No animal in the wild, suddenly overcome with fear, would spend any of its mental energy thinking, 'It's probably nothing.'"[11]

De Becker said, "Intuition is the journey from A to Z without stopping at any other letter along the way. It is knowing without

---

10. Gavin De Becker, *The Gift of Fear* (New York, NY: Dell Publishing, 1997), 24–25.
11. De Becker, *The Gift of Fear*, 29–30.

knowing why." We don't need to know the why; we just need to trust the life-giving signals that alert us to ongoings in our lives.

While De Becker speaks about the use of intuition to keep us out of deadly situations, I'm referring to intuition as a way to open our hearts to the things that live within—to completely open to ourselves, every bit, and to trust in the signals that come our way, whether in a lifesaving situation, resurrecting a relationship, or most importantly, our own life resuscitation.

Whether your intuition adamantly signals that you are in danger, something is off in your marriage, a decision is wrong, or something is not right with your child, trust it, and don't let logic reason it away.

Intuition can help us know good truths too. The blind man in the Bible who cried out for Jesus's help wasn't so blind. As Jesus walked by, the man felt the presence of the Son of God. His intuition knew that Holiness had brushed past him, and he wouldn't let it escape. He acted upon his inner knowledge, crying out from the depth of his soul, and stopped Jesus in His tracks. He trusted what he felt, and his life path shifted. That's the power of intuition—it changes everything.

Finally, redeveloping intuition is vital because it affects all areas in our lives—our safety, relationships, decisions, and spiritual matters.

I started listening closely to my inner voice and acknowledging it. I deciphered if it was a brief feeling or a persistent intuitive signal warning me of something greater. If it was a feeling, I'd deal with it. If it was my intuition, I'd linger there, trusting and figuring out what deeper things needed to be addressed.

When focusing on my inner guide, I assessed if there was a safety issue that presented itself. Sometimes, it was something someone said in one of my relationships that told me there were deeper things involved. Other times, it was a business situation that seemed off and needed me to look at it closer. Maybe it was a signal for prayer in someone else's life (like Caston's scenario) or a confrontation that needed to take place. More often than not, it surrounded the areas in my life that required continual prayer and spiritual attention.

In my daily life, I was able to see things in a new light and apply intuition in every area. If I ever had another similar open house, it'd be handled differently. The minute I felt that slight warning from the aggressive knock on the door, I'd trust my intuition. And when I got to the front door, instead of opening it, I'd lock it and call for help. I wouldn't question or judge my reasoning; I'd simply stand firm in what my body said, and that action alone would be a day changer.

"The truth remains that your safety is yours. It is not the responsibility of the police, the government, industry, the apartment building manager, or the security company."[12]

What could it have looked like in that decade of winter with David? I just knew something wasn't right with him. I'd get pangs in my gut when something was said or when we were in certain situations. My body yelled at me, but I kept denying it.

When I felt that first twinge in my gut that something was off in my marriage, I should've first listened to it and then addressed it. I should've said, "Hold up, what you just said (or did) doesn't feel right. What's going on? Talk to me," or, "I'm not going to receive that," or, "How can I help?"

Perhaps it's an intuitive feeling that something isn't right with a child. In acting on that, someone might say, "I want you to feel like you can trust me with your heart. It seems like you have something

---

12. De Becker, *The Gift of Fear*, 10.

that's bothering you. How can I come alongside you and support you through this?"

When something feels suspicious with a stranger, an employee, the girlfriend who's obsessively calling, the neighbor, the babysitter, the schoolteacher, a relative, or someone who walks into an open house, give yourself the gift of listening to your intuition and let it safely guide you. Trust it implicitly, and act on what it's telling you to do. That's how you receive. And you'll grasp more of God and receive the best of yourself.

Since opening my heart to my inner wisdom, I've avoided disastrous decisions and dangers, strengthening myself to make the next right choice. In listening to my inner voice, I've experienced the peace of God that surpasses all understanding.

As I developed my inner compass, it directed my steps and taught me to trust His lead. It also trained me to trust my own lead. I became more equipped in managing my feelings and believing in my intuitive signals, which empowered me to open my heart and continually become more steadfast.

Trusting my intuition gave me the freedom to accept it without judgment. I no longer ignored it or shut it down because I was no longer afraid I'd accidentally "call into being things that were not" (Romans 4:17 [NIV]). I realized God gave us intuition not only as a gift to show us good things, but most importantly, to warn us of situations and allow us to partner with Him in heavenly battles.

That's how we ultimately receive from ourselves. We believe so deeply that "God Under There" directs our lives and sends signals for us to obey. Once we lean into this God-given gift, we honor ourselves by listening and acting on it, and it changes everything—shifting the atmosphere of our lives. Intuition can save our relationships with ourselves and with others.

I was as ready as I could be to receive and *receive not*, empowered to have the purest relationships possible with God, myself, and others.

It was so life-giving. I felt freer and more confident as I started connecting with David on a deeper level than we'd ever experienced in our thirty-five years together. It was good because I was receiving me.

The biggest lesson I learned in accepting my intuition was realizing that by leaning into it, I was receiving from the Holy Spirit who lives within.

I no longer traversed through life alone; I experienced life with Him by receiving His direction. And His lead is always best.

12

Practice Two – Drop the Weight

I will come again and conquer you
because as a mountain you can't grow,
but as a human, I can.
—Sir Edmund Hillary

MY TREK WASN'T ONLY A WILDERNESS TIME, BUT ALSO A TIME of discovery and healing. It'd been a treacherous journey—one I wouldn't want to take again, but one that grew me into a better version of who I used to be.

I suppose that's how one discovers the deepest beauty within—by making an expedition up the mountain of life, through sudden wild storms and rockslides. I'd either reach the summit or die trying, but I hadn't given up, and for that I was proud.

I kept on. I stayed focused.

The effects of my climb took their toll. I needed to rest and pause if only for a day. I took a morning to reflect on where I'd been and where I was headed, and I let my imaginary backpack slip down my arms and tumble onto the ground. As I exhaled, I realized then the tremendous weight I'd been carrying for so long.

When did I let this weight become comfortable?

I'll own the fact that I chose to carry those things—things I believed about myself and things other people stuffed into my backpack. Packed full, I couldn't completely recall all that was tucked inside.

I crouched and took a seat next to my stuff. I noticed the familiar friend had become worn from the journey as I ran my finger across the opening. It'd seen better days and looked the way I felt.

Why had I chosen to feel comforted by what I packed deeply within?

Somehow, the contents stirred my emotions and kept me going, helping me feel alive—even if they were unhealthy for me to carry.

I faced a choice in that moment. I could keep fueling my "aliveness" with the drama of the dead weight or let it go.

Sometimes, we don't want to release the heavy things. We drag them along and even guard them, but if we don't let them go, we might just die trying to reach our summits.

All the things I believed about myself messed with my mind, reached my heart, and penetrated my soul. The result? A hardness that kept me closed up and not open to receive or reject.

Without shedding the heavy load, I probably wouldn't have reached the top of my mountain. The rocks of my past had to go, and I knew it was time to drop the weight.

I unzipped the backpack, brave enough to peek, and slipped my hand inside to feel for the first cool rock. I quickly let it go and heard it smack the rocks beneath it. If I emptied it right there, what proof would I have that it all took place? Most importantly, if I discarded all that stuff, would I still feel alive? What would stir me to keep going? I wouldn't know until I faced it.

The path of uncertainty stretched out before me. It would've been more comfortable to simply pick up my backpack and keep trekking. Besides, I was used to its load. Temptation to continue my journey the way I had all my life swirled around me. People want change but not the unease to get there, and I wasn't any different. Yet, I stayed put.

I closed my eyes, found the courage to reach inside again, and slowly pulled out a rock. I gave myself permission to look and exhaled in defeat.

"Hello," I whispered.

With great sadness, I read the three words that were written: *waste of time.*

How long had I felt like a waste of time? Or did I feel like I had wasted time? Perhaps it was both. Regardless, I felt tormented by those words.

What other things lay waiting for me inside the backpack?

And could I face them all at once?

I held on tightly to the rock. My mind drifted to a story in the Bible about a man who was possessed.

I wondered, *How long did he live with this torment?*

Yeshua and his *talmidim* arrived at the other side of the lake, in the Gerasenes territory. As soon as he disembarked, a man with an unclean spirit came out of the burial caves to meet him. He lived in the burial caves; and no one could keep him tied up, not even with a chain. He had often been chained hand and foot, but he would snap the chains and break the irons off his feet, and no one was strong enough to control him. Night and day he wandered among the graves and through the hills, howling and gashing himself with stones. Seeing Yeshua from a distance, he ran and fell on his knees in front of him and screamed at the top of his voice, "What do you want with me, Yeshua, Son of God *Ha'Elyon*? I implore you in God's name! Don't torture me!" For Yeshua had already begun saying to him, "Unclean spirit, come out of this man!" Yeshua asked him, "What's your name?" "My name is Legion," he answered, "there are so many of us"; and he kept begging Yeshua not to send them out of that region. Now there was a large herd of pigs feeding near the hill, and the unclean spirits begged him, "Send us to the pigs, so we can go into them." Yeshua gave them permission. They came out and entered the pigs; and the herd, numbering around two thousand, rushed down the hillside into the lake and were drowned. (Mark 5:1–13 [CJB])

The question Jesus asked lingered with me.

"What's your name?"

The demon-filled man's name was Legion, meaning there are so many of us.

The man was tortured by many names; perhaps just like him, I needed to get rid of the things that tortured me. I needed to perform an exorcism and drown the names I'd been weighted down with.

As Jesus spoke to the unclean spirits, the man was set free, and after that, he sat there, dressed and in his right mind.

I needed Jesus to speak to my demons—the rocks that falsely labeled me and kept me bound.

Could it be that simple?

Is it possible that, upon hearing Jesus's truth, the unclean spirits of my own torment would just…flee?

Well, I'm made in God's image, and His truth, spoken through me, has power—doesn't it? I pondered what might happen if I spoke to what was haunting me.

I thought about holding that imaginary rock in my hand, running my finger over the rough surface, and looking at a lake before me.

I imagined the man's relief as he finally became free. And then, I heard that gentle voice of God within saying, *Nothing is wasted in my kingdom.*

Those words filled me with strength. Just like the man filled with unclean spirits, I cried out at the top of my voice, "Nothing is wasted in God's kingdom!" With all of my might, I threw the rock into the lake and saw in my mind's eye the splash of the water.

Waste of time was gone.

I took a deep breath. Was all that had transpired in my life wasted? *No.*

Then I remembered the line from the book *Modoc*: "The past gives us our strength, so to be sad about gaining strength is not very wise, is it?"[13]

I reached in again and felt so many rocks, so I picked up a small one with a big word on it that said *shameful.* I recited the scripture. "Don't be afraid, for you won't be ashamed; don't be discouraged, for you won't be disgraced. You will forget the shame of your youth" (Isaiah 54:4 [CJB]).

I chucked the shameful rock into the water as a tear ran down my face. *Kerplop!* And it was gone. Did God give me a spirit of shame? No. I was free to no longer carry that burden.

I reached into my backpack and pulled out the next rock. It read, *abandoned.*

I thought about one particular night where I was left alone. Then, His voice came to me and said, *I will never leave you nor forsake you.* As I thought more on that cold night, I remembered the

---

13. Ralph Helfer, *Modoc: The True Story of the Greatest Elephant That Ever Lived* (New York, NY: Harper Collins, 1997), 275.

presence of God so strongly. He'd been there. He never left. I threw the rock, and it skipped once before it disappeared into the water. God has always been with me.

The next rock was like a close friend to me. Holding onto it, I remembered how long it had traveled with me. It read, *never good enough.*

"Goodbye, old friend. You've lied to me all these years, and I falsely believed you. We can no longer hang out. God says I'm more than enough," I said and pitched it into the water. It was gone in an instant.

The next rock surprised me. I thought I had pretty good self-esteem, but I've felt this way at times. It said, *worthless.*

But what does God say I am? God says I'm priceless. I yelled as I ditched the rock into the water. "I'm priceless!" Then all I heard was the splash.

It was getting easier to look at what had been weighing me down and discard it.

The next rock read, *damaged.*

Except I knew from the story of the demon-possessed man that he didn't allow himself to feel damaged. Instead, scripture says this after he was healed: "He went off and began proclaiming in the Ten Towns how much Yeshua had done for him, and everyone was amazed" (Mark 5:20 [CJB]).

That man didn't let his past define him. Once he was healed and in his right mind, he shared the good news with those he encountered. I'd do the same. I didn't let the label "damaged" stay with me long, so I threw the rock into the lake.

As my hand made its way inside the backpack again, I was surprised to find more rocks.

I thought, *How was I able to carry this for so many years? And how did it feel so natural to lug around?*

Picking up another rock, I flipped it over to see what I needed to be rid of next: *alone*.

I used to feel like everything was always up to me; if I don't do it, it won't get done. Responsible Dawna—there she was again. Except that untruth faded quickly as God whispered to me, "Are you tired? Worn out? Burned out on religion? Come to me. Get away with me and you'll recover your life. I'll show you how to take a real rest. Walk with me and work with me—watch how I do it. Learn the unforced rhythms of grace. I won't lay anything heavy or ill-fitting on you. Keep company with me and you'll learn to live freely and lightly" (Matthew 11:28–30 [MSG]).

I thought about all the times God was with me and all the miracles I'd seen Him perform. When I was truthful with myself, it was Him who got things done. I did my part, but without God's help, I never would've gotten things completely right.

Believing I was alone was a lie, so I hurled the rock into the lake. Then I whispered, "Thank you, God, for all Your miracles. I'm never alone. I have You."

Lifting the pack, I realized how much lighter it was. Still, there were a few more things to deal with. So, I picked up an oblong rock that read, *lost cause*.

I thought about all the encounters that Jesus had with so many. No one and nothing seemed to be a lost cause. He always sought out the broken and spoke words of life to them. He went to those who were lost and helped them find themselves.

I wound this one up and pitched it into the lake as if attempting to strike out a batter. As it flew through the air, my soul soared with encouraging thoughts. *No one is a lost cause. No matter how much discouragement sets in, He's working all things together for good. He's making me new through all of it.* I was so caught up in my thoughts that I didn't hear the splash of the water.

Next was a small stone in my hand that read, *failure.*

I thought about all my disappointments, and a quote came to mind: "I hope I outlive my regrets."[14]

As I inhaled the truth of that statement, I thought back to when I first became a real estate agent. Inexperienced, I didn't know much and made some mistakes along the way. However, those mishaps stuck with me longer than the successes, and they drove me to do my very best. They were reminders of how to do things more skillfully, and I'm a better agent today because of them.

Suddenly, my life's failures faded. I realized that my own mishaps shaped me into the person standing by the lake that day. I liked who I'd become throughout my journey, so I decided not to let my insufficiencies linger any longer.

I turned my hand over and let the rock drop into the water. It hit the shallow surface and rolled deeper and deeper until I couldn't see it anymore.

Searching the pack, I found one last rock that read, *nobody.*

For years, I allowed that one to bum around, knowing it was a bold-faced lie.

Why did I give it a free ride?

In God's eyes, we're all *somebody.* He designed each of us with unique talents and gifts. I am somebody. Knowing that, I tossed the rock into the water as if throwing an underhand ball, and it was gone.

With an empty backpack, I'd dropped the weight of my torment. Jesus calls us to live a life free of torment and to quit letting labeled rocks define us. Perhaps like me, it's time to forgive yourself and accept deliverance.

Can you name your "rocks" right now?

---

14. Bob Logan, *Not Quite What I Was Planning* (Harper Collins, 2008), 26.

Do you know they're keeping you from reaching your own mountain summit?

Receive yourself. Be open to the possibility of an improved you. To do this, you can't be ruled by the things of the past that hold you down. Dropping the weight of the stuff in your backpack will free your mind, heart, and soul. Give yourself the grace to let it all go and start anew.

While the man in Mark 5:1–13 was literally possessed by demons, our childhood giants can be used against us by our adversary, Satan, to lie, torment, and keep us bound in chains. Burdened with the backpack of untruth, we discover we're carrying our past. Even though we put to death the giants that taunt us, we choose to drag them along.

I'd slayed my giants, but up until this point, I hadn't realized I was still encumbered. I needed to let go. I used the same model that Jesus did when He overcame Satan's various temptations in the wilderness—by speaking God's truth. He didn't argue with Satan; He simply confessed God's word, and Satan fled. So, I tossed the labeled rocks into God's lake of grace. I confessed the truths of who God says I am:

Accomplished.
Rediscovered.
More than enough.
Irreplaceable and cherished.
Renewed.
Encouraged.
Confident.
Strong.
Somebody.

I chose to be fueled and feel alive by the truths that God spoke about me. I decided to look at the past with a new promise; God made me better through it. I acknowledged who I'd become and focused on where I was headed. Everything I've experienced led me to become a stronger woman.

Once we've received our anointing, questioned and declared, and run toward our enemy, we still must remember, like King David, to sling the stone.

When Sir Edmund Hillary led the first expedition up Mount Everest, an unexpected storm swept through, and many on the trek died. Sir Edmund Hillary, in great defeat, returned home.

At a planning meeting to attempt the climb again, he looked at a picture of Mount Everest and said, "I will come again and conquer you because as a mountain you can't grow, but as a human, I can."

Sir Edmund Hillary eventually climbed Mount Everest again and was the first to officially reach the mountain's summit.

Similarly, we must trek on in life. We'll never reach perfection if we live at base camp. Climbing helps attain who we're created to be.

My trek wasn't a physical mountain, but rather a spiritual journey. It felt like I wandered through a dry desert season only to discover I stood at the base of the mountain I never dreamed I'd be asked to climb.

I've never physically hiked a mountain—I'm more of a water-girl-I'll-cheer-you-on kind of gal. You climb, and I'll meet you on the other side as your refreshing encourager.

Sir Edmund Hillary said, "It is not the mountains we conquer but ourselves…we conquer ourselves little by little, as in climbing up a high mountain: 'Come, and let us go up to the mountain of the Lord.'"[15]

I trekked through an emotional desert and climbed a mountain through a season of loss.

Before I reached the summit, however, I had to empty my backpack for the final ascent. Making my climb with a lighter load, I was able to appreciate all I'd left behind. While God didn't erase the memories of the past, He helped me see that every unexpected storm, landslide, avalanche, and setback aided my journey to self-conquer and become the strongest version of myself.

I decided to use each painful memory that came to mind as a healthy reminder of where I'd been and how far I'd come. I thought, *I'm wiser now. I won't go that way again.* And then I was free to look ahead and not behind.

I made a conscious decision to focus on the miracles I'd seen. I chose to love who I'd become—someone better from the journey. I'd climbed the mountain of the Lord, and I *received* myself completely.

I was strong enough to sling my stones.

---

15. "It Is Not the Mountain We Conquer, But Ourselves," Quote Investigator, last modified August 18, 2016, https://quoteinvestigator.com/2016/08/18/conquer/#more-14308.

13

Practice Three – The Heart's Motivation

The fact that our heart yearns for
something Earth can't supply is proof
that Heaven must be our home.
—C.S. Lewis

WHILE THE FIRST TWO PRACTICES FOCUSED ON THE MIND, THE next three will deal with the heart. I learned about the heart's motivation in Israel.

Israel was a turning point for me.

Standing on holy ground, the Bible stories came to life. With a new understanding of the setting, culture, Hebrew meanings, archaeology, and history, a deeper comprehension took root.

One of the lessons I learned while visiting the City of David was the ultimate receive from God—accepting all that He has for me then implementing change. There was a dimension to me that I never truly allowed myself to look at, but embracing God's plan helped me become strong enough to examine my own heart's motivation as honestly as I could.

Revealing my inner motives was a difficult practice, but just "seeing and understanding" wasn't enough. If I truly expected to open my heart, I needed to take action. Finding the best version of myself was the most loving thing I could do.

While it's not easy, it's worth it.

My trip to the holy land was exhausting. It was a bucket-list trip for me, yet at times, I was irritable. There were huge crowds of people, early-morning and late-night bus rides, and constant rushing from place to place that stole my fantasies of a peace-filled spiritual journey.

We're not supposed to blaze through big moments like that, but we had to if we wanted to see everything on the itinerary. It felt like there was no room for the unexpected.

Still, in all the hurry throughout Israel, I experienced some profound moments. I saw and recognized areas of my heart that God expected me to work on with Him in my becoming anew.

Running through Israel tired and emotional felt similar to when I started implementing things that helped me accept the good and reject the unhealthy. While applying the two practices of the mind seemed challenging enough, dealing with heart issues seemed more so. I discovered stuff in my own heart that brought me to tears—some from hard stories and others from the joyful and sweet moments.

Every snapshot of my life was layered just like the ancient ruins of Israel's land. It's a lot of work to unearth, and holy mackerel, I had a lot of digging to do. As tiring as it was, employing those newly discovered practices was like brushing away the dirt to uncover beautiful ancient cities. I had to keep revealing the best parts of me.

Once you see and employ the coming practices, you'll feel I'm crowding in on your space. You'll be pressed to push yourself harder than you thought possible. You'll feel tired, frustrated, and like someone stole your fantasy of what you thought enlightenment should be.

People don't change unless they're uncomfortable. And while discomfort doesn't sound inviting, it truly is the stepping-stone to a new way of living freely.

Hang in there as the trek gets tougher. I promise you'll experience profound moments and start loving the way you healthily receive and reject. It's vital to implement these new strategies so you can rewrite your own legacies and transform into the strongest version of yourself.

As your tour guide, I'll help you through them. And as you employ each one, take some time to rest and reflect.

When I was in Israel, there were times I ran to keep up with the tour, learning and gleaning as much as I could. However, I also chose to step away when I needed to reflect and leave some room for the unexpected. Rather than having dinner with the group every night, I sometimes departed early to process the day and journal my thoughts. I left an ancient synagogue right in the middle of worship to walk along the ancient tombs and sing solo to God. One day, David and I ditched the tour group altogether to walk through the markets of Jerusalem and emerge ourselves in the culture.

As you read each practice, take a day to explore it. Allow your heart's motivation to move, inform, guide, and teach you more about yourself. Once you're ready, move on to the next practice. Let the journey take its time—neither too rushed nor too slow—and open your heart to change. Let them both push you to see all that your heart is capable of, both good and bad, and allow your heart to become a place for you to discover yourself anew and become more alive, aware, and in awe of how complex you really are.

* * *

The heart can both lead and mislead us; that's why scripture says to guard it. "Above everything else, guard your heart; for it is the source of life's consequences" (Proverbs 4:23 [CJB]).

When our heart is full of the wrong things, it can lead us down a sketchy path. Too many times I've allowed it to take me where I wasn't meant to go. So, I learned to guard it and guide it down the right path. Understanding the heart's true motivation is important.

By protecting my own heart and opening it to receive goodness, I discerned what I'm really capable of. While identifying my inner motives, I fell in love with the person who was pinpointing them—me!

One particular instance happened when I was forced to look at my own heart's motivation about a situation revealed to me over coffee with Carla.

Even while driving to meet Carla, I knew something brewed on the inside. I needed her to be my sounding board. I was pretty good at assessing what I struggled with, which I haven't always been, but I discovered what was happening on the inside when I talked about it with guidance from a trusted adviser.

I shared with Carla that I was mentoring a younger woman— someone God unexpectedly brought into my life. My initial meeting with her was pure surface talk, but it swiftly got deeper. I told Carla how inadequate I felt to give any advice, and I questioned, *Am I even supposed to?*

I heard myself rattling off all my fears to Carla—all the ways I failed to say the right thing, was unable to point toward God, and only listened and embraced. Wasn't I supposed to have some great spiritual direction to offer? I felt a pressure to have all the answers and yet felt completely ill-equipped for the job.

More neurotic than ever, I rummaged through my purse, looking for my lavender essential oil because I needed to *calm down*. But I kept going on about how it felt like a huge responsibility. Someday, I would stand before God and answer for my role in what I said or didn't say in speaking into this person's life. After all, God's word tells us that if we teach and lead, we'll be held at a higher standard than others.

Carla didn't know the name of the young woman or her story. I just told her some general information because I'm passionate about not sharing someone's past and holding onto those stories in a sacred place. Carla offered me a soothing smile as unshakable as the throne of God and a safe haven to share my overwhelming energy.

I desperately searched for the calming oil in the crevices of my purse. When I finally found it, I dabbed some behind my ears and said, "What if I mess this up?"

As if speaking with an angel, Carla calmly replied, "You're being a sanctuary."

"Yes, but it feels like by listening, I'm agreeing with her."

"Has she asked for your advice?"

"No. She just shared her story. But aren't we all called to gently guide and point toward God?"

Carla shook her head. "I don't believe so—not unless God specifically directs you to *and* only if that person asks for your advice."

"Are you sure about this? We're called to be witnesses."

"True, but only if the person is ready to receive," Carla said.

Receive. That was it. Each of us needed to be open to receive, and if someone wasn't ready, we'd just remain present and listen.

Carla affirmed me. "What you're describing—the way you've responded to this young woman—reminds me of Jesus. He safely sat alongside others and offered sheltered spaces. Initially in His conversations, all Jesus did was ask questions."

I thought of Jesus's encounters in the scriptures, and a peace settled in my soul.

Jesus operated that way, and the more I mirrored Him coming alongside others and not attempting to fix their situations or insert God into their lives, the more I saw God in the midst. Many times, just hearing someone—truly listening without an agenda—brought about their own enlightenment because there's healing in being heard.

Carla resumed. "Jesus sat with the woman at the well and had a discussion. He asked important questions that stirred her heart and made her want more of God, not less. Jesus is a sanctuary who sits beside us throughout our struggles and asks our hearts the right questions. That's what you're doing, Dawna!"

I blinked, taking in her words. I've mentored many women but haven't felt like *that* before, so why was I so anxious over that particular young woman?

"You're right, Carla. I *am* being a safe space. There must be something deeper to what I'm feeling. I've been developing a theory about our heart's motivations. What I've discovered is that when we can understand what we're feeling, we'll discover that our heart has hidden motivations. I'm anxious about my visit with this woman, but I'm uncertain as to why."

Carla held her coffee cup with both hands and leaned in. "Wow! That's interesting. What do you think your heart's motivation is in this situation?"

"I'm not sure yet. But as it unfolds, I'll share more. What I know right now is that we as women need to come alongside other women more, meet them where they are, and be a resting place for others. While we sit next to others and listen to their stories, we need to search within to discover our own hidden agendas and address them before we attempt to offer anyone else advice. That's as far as I've gotten. But now, recognizing my anxiety, I see that I need to search within. Oh my goodness! Thanks so much for helping me."

Carla laughed. "I don't feel like I did anything; you've fleshed this out yourself."

I left knowing I'd chosen a great listener to help me. The good listening wisdom of a trusted friend will always bring truth to the heart. After talking with Carla, I realized that I was on the right track, but something deeper needed my attention. I just couldn't figure out what.

Heart-Stirring Questions

My beginning step to discover my heart's motivation was to develop a deeper understanding of myself by listening within and clarifying what was really going on.

When I felt uncomfortable during my mentoring sessions with the young woman, I knew that was my first sign. Before pressing on with the conversation and then running to Carla to help clarify my feelings, I should've paused in the moment to take note of my unease.

Once in tune with myself, I could inquire within. *I'm feeling uneasy here. Why?*

Understanding my inner reactions helped me deal with my own heart first. If I have a self-motivated response to someone or a comeback triggered by internal wrestling, I'm not at a point where I can objectively advise or help anyone.

Ask questions that gracefully call yourself out. Hold yourself accountable for your thoughts, feelings, and the way you communicate. You can't receive from others or give to them if you're not open and honest with yourself first. Heart-stirring questions begin within.

Later that day, I thought back to the conversation with the young woman in an attempt to get a better understanding on my own discomfort. The more I thought about it, the more I realized why I was so anxious. My meeting with her was actually my first true attempt to *not* fix anything and simply sit with someone in their suffering. It was painful to do, say, and repair nothing. It felt awkward.

Wanting to help someone isn't a bad thing, but it can be if the heart isn't in the right place. I must be a hero to myself before I can rescue anyone else.

The uncertainty that followed my meeting wasn't about messing up how I responded to her; that was just the surface. It went deeper than that to a level of discomfort that triggered me. My heart's motivation was revealed—quit fixing and be present.

Identifying that was like unearthing a city hidden beneath. I got a glimpse of the first roof tile exposed from the underground city, and I felt my need to fix emerge. *Why did this seem so difficult?*

The best way to check the heart's motivation is to ask God.

The next morning, I sat propped up in bed for some alone time with Him. My heart was slow to reveal itself, so I gently whispered, "Why do I feel the need to make everything right? What is this need to help everyone?"

I felt the sweet presence of mercy beside me.

"Lord, reveal to me my heart's motivation."

Silence. He never rushed with answers, so I continued. "What do you want me to know about myself? About this situation? About my own heart?"

Still nothing. God didn't squirm at my impatience.

"I just want those I care about to be all right."

I imagined Jesus sitting next to me and scooting closer. Sitting side by side, I placed my head on His imaginary shoulder as tears slid down my cheeks.

Like a gentle summer breeze, His voice swept through my mind. "I've placed eternity in your heart. You long for it."

That was a true statement; how I longed for all to be made right.

I acknowledged His truth as he went on. "Dawna, you long for love stories, miracles, and happy endings. You want the risen Savior on Easter morning, but not the suffering perfection of the crucifixion. Your soul doesn't mature when everything is easy—it becomes strengthened in me in the hard places of trials and pain. You can trust me and let go of *fixing*. Make room for the growth I'm inviting you into. Besides, I'm the only One who redeems all things."

I scoffed at His words. "This 'growth' hasn't felt inviting—it feels difficult. And yes, I long to make things right."

He let me sit with my frustration before another whisper came. "Attempting to fix someone's situation doesn't redeem your own."

Conviction gently washed over me.

True, my heart honestly longed to help the young woman. But what if by helping make her situation right, I somehow believed I could revise or even lessen the sting of my own season of loss?

"Dawna, my dear, quit trying to rewrite your own receptive story. Give me back the pen."

God was correct, but his truth had to sink in before I responded. I thought about the last ten years and how I'd trusted him, yet I'd given way to my own impatience. I longed for the perfection of Eden and, at times, crafted my own narrative in an attempt to get there.

"Oh, Lord, forgive me. You're so right. I hand my story back over to you."

A sense of relief washed over me as the weight lifted, and I whispered six words to Jesus: "Decade of winter, please initiate spring."

His presence lingered even though I didn't hear another word.

That day, God revealed my heart's motivation. I wanted so desperately to make my own story have meaning that I somehow falsely believed that by helping someone else, I'd feel better about my own journey.

I finally understood how to identify deeper things and give myself the freedom to let go, detach from desperately needing to help, be right, or lead someone to see things my way, which only covered up what was really going on inside. Helping someone through their problems wouldn't revise my own history. And I can't properly help until my heart's motivation is pure.

God doesn't call us to fix others. He calls us to fix ourselves, and it was time to fix myself.

He called me out and showed me that my manipulations weren't satisfying. He's the only one who can make all things new again, which is why it's so important to uncover what's truly lurking in my heart every day.

Listening to what's going on within is a crucial indicator to deeper yearnings. It helped me address my inner issues and not project them onto others. By identifying my own unease, I dug deeper and gave myself room to probe my heart. In turn, it headed off on my own agenda, helped me withhold *my* beliefs, and steered the conversation in a neutral direction.

My job was to sit safely beside the woman and let her share what was in her heart—whether or not I agreed and without trying to fix anything. Being present and creating a safe place meant she was free to share and, hopefully in the future, free to *receive* from me—if she asked.

So, what heart-stirring questions could I have asked myself during my time with the young woman? What heart-stirring questions could I have asked her?

Here are some things I could've asked myself:

- "Why am I so eager to contain this conversation?"

- "I feel uncomfortable. Why is that?"

- "In what ways can I identify with her story?"

- "In what ways do I *not* want to identify with her story?"

- "What childhood giant would be most uncomfortable here?"

Here are some things I could've asked her:

- "Can you identify what you need in this moment?"

- "How do you know this is the path you're supposed to take?"

- "Is it possible that there's something deeper within to take note of?"

- "How do you see yourself moving forward?"

- "How can I pray for you?"

I must honor myself and *receive* what's inside me so I can become the truest version of myself and allow God to unearth all that's hidden within. I'll admit I haven't been as successful as I'd like, but I'm constantly working on it.

When David lost his identity in the great recession, I told him all the things *I thought* he needed to hear to get back in the game.

"Get your mind right."

"Your identity is not a builder."

"Get over it."

Those unhelpful phrases only wedged us further apart because it wasn't what he needed to hear at the time. He didn't need me to fix him; he needed me to listen. And I couldn't listen if my heart had its own agenda.

Hidden in my heart was fear. *What if David never returns to his old self—the man I married and loved so much? What if he never recovers and I have to figure out life on my own?*

I couldn't look at my heart's worry. So, to shut it down, I gave short answers and grew angry. I didn't "guard my heart" but allowed it to travel the sketchy path of fear.

If I would've had the courage and the know-how, perhaps I could've questioned myself with the following heart-stirring questions:

- "What scares you about David not recovering?"

- "What do you need in order to be okay if he doesn't recover?"

- "What kind of wife do you want to be?"

Once strong enough to know what stirred on the inside, I could address it and get myself to a healthy place. I could identify what I needed and take care of myself. Only then was I capable of caring for and advising David.

Some questions I should've asked David are:

- "What can I do for you right now?"

- "Will you please help me make this decision?"

- "Will you come with me to counseling?"

In receiving my heart's concern that David might never be the same—that *we'd* never be the same—I could've dealt with our situation in a more productive way. It would've at least changed *me* and *my* well-being. And that's all I can do.

Asking heart-stirring questions is vital to one's own well-being because it reveals the inner workings of the heart. Digging for my heart's motivation helped me discover I was attempting to edit my own story. It also showed me that at times during my wilderness decade, I gave in to fear.

Hidden deep within were self-motivations that hindered my ability to love someone like Jesus does. At times, my heart still doesn't want to deal with my own issues; they're too difficult to even look at, let alone correct, but now I push myself. Perhaps that's why Jesus said, "First take the plank out of your own eye, and then you will see clearly to remove the speck from your brother's eye" (Matthew 7:5 [NIV]).

Our heart's motivations need to be identified, evaluated honestly, and modified through God's Spirit. *Then, and only then*, are we ready to speak truth powerfully to those God placed in our lives.

What misguided motives do you sense right now?

Would you take a few moments to sit with them and perhaps journal about what you're feeling?

As C.S. Lewis said, "The fact that our heart yearns for something Earth can't supply is proof that Heaven must be our home." Our hearts yearn for all things to be right. Of course it does. We were created to live in perfect harmony with God, not in the upside-down world we currently dwell in. But until things are made new, it's up to us to get our own hearts right. To identify our motivations and direct them accordingly. It's not our job to get someone else's heart right; God expects us to tend to our own.

Life's assaults had buried my heart. Discovering my own motives helped uncover the truest me and freed me to begin to love like Jesus. Looking back, I didn't have a hold on myself, and because of that, I couldn't possibly have a good grasp on my relationships.

David had me, my mom had me, and my friends had me, but Dawna didn't have herself. It was time for me to release everyone else's grasp and take hold of myself.

Once I understood myself in a truer light, I could more readily find my deepest inner workings and implement the changes God intended for my life before speaking to someone else's.

I became acquainted with myself, receiving the fullness of who I'd grown into throughout the desert journey. This time had created a strength planted deep within. God made me into a true warrior— one who learned to receive and receive not—and it was beautiful. Not only was I stronger, David and I were more connected than ever.

This experienced soldier was confident. No one had ever seen that side of me—including myself.

So, the next time I met with the young woman, I felt a new sense of peace. I knew without a doubt I was called to sit beside her and listen. I wasn't supposed to fix anything except myself.

I understood my own heart's motivations and addressed them one at a time as they presented themselves. And my heart only felt lighter.

14

Practice Four –
Welcome Those Around the Table

Emotions are celebrated and repressed,
analyzed and medicated, adored and ignored
—but rarely, if ever, are they honored.
—Karla McLaren

THE MIND AND HEART ARE INTERNALLY CONNECTED; EVEN THOUGH they're two separate organs, they affect each other.

The Bible tells us that what we think goes straight to the heart. That's why it's so important to be the protectors of our minds and guard our hearts because what originates in thought takes residency in the heart. Eventually, we speak what we believe, and that spoken word plays out on the stage of our lives.

"But what comes out of your mouth is actually coming from your heart, and that is what makes a person unclean. For out of the heart come forth wicked thoughts, murder, adultery and other kinds of sexual immorality, theft, lies, slanders" (Matthew 15:18–19 [CJB]).

"Above everything else, guard your heart; for it is the source of life's consequences" (Proverbs 4:23 [CJB]).

My thoughts made their way to my heart and mouth, shaping

my reality. With God's assistance, I held the power to shift my own outcomes.

I wondered if, when I shut down my intuition, I suppressed my feelings at the same time. At that point in my journey, I didn't like emotions. I falsely believed that if I didn't give in to feelings, I wouldn't have to deal with my issues that surrounded them. But shutting out what I felt didn't make my problems disappear; they simply compounded within and eventually altered my heart and life.

As young girls, we're taught to deflect our feelings. We're supposed to be polite, act like a lady, and stay quiet despite how we feel. Young boys learn that it's not "manly" to reveal their emotions, and if they do, they'll show weakness, not masculinity.

We've adopted these false narratives and carried them into our adult lives, many times to our own detriment. Why is it frowned upon to state unease with someone or a situation as a young lady? And why can't men cry and be strong at the same time? Many of us have accepted these untruths and repressed our innermost feelings.

This was true even in my family. We didn't discuss our feelings because they made others in the house uncomfortable. So, we repressed them instead. Because we couldn't talk about feelings or process issues within our immediate family—my mom, dad, and sister—we most certainly didn't share with others our personal life or the ongoings of our home. Telling others our problems in paradise was forbidden.

Growing up, I'd be dismissed or reprimanded for expressing how I felt. If I was overcome by feelings of loneliness, I'd get a hasty reminder that I had family members residing in our home and I *shouldn't* feel lonely. I was asked, "How can you feel like that?"

I truly didn't know how I *could* feel like that; I just did. Without the freedom to explore how I felt and why, I began hiding it all. If I got emotional, I'd apologize. Somewhere along the way, I became a stoic young woman who wasn't an "emotional girl," and I was proud of my own insensitivity.

By not honoring our feelings, we suppress and numb the heart, eventually hardening it. At some point, suppression will reveal itself in one form or another. Try all you like, but pressed-down feelings resurface in the most unusual ways and at the most inconvenient times. Listening closely to your feelings is essential.

Unfortunately, many of us don't accept and validate our deepest feelings until much later in life. I'm just now discovering how to do this. It took the discomfort of my own life to uncover my repression. Fortunately, through wisdom and guidance from my therapist, I was able to uncover deep truths within.

I hadn't realized how numb I'd become to my inner self. By shutting down, I was dying inside. So, I had to begin tuning in to how I felt to revive my heart.

I discovered some truths:

- *My feelings are valid even if they make others uncomfortable.*

- *My feelings are valid even if they don't make sense.*

- *My feelings are valid, and I don't have to justify them.*

- And my favorite one: *others can't tell you how you feel.*

Inquiring within, I discovered my feelings have individual "personalities," each one being birthed through life experiences and with specific purposes for me. Among my own inner voices were two others: the voice of the enemy of our souls, Satan, and the more powerful and one true voice I could trust, God.

I began identifying my own voices and started to see that every personality gave important signals: warnings, fears, wisdom, spiritual direction, and paths to take and not take, and it all began by identifying and acknowledging those sitting around my inner table.

So, who lived inside?

Identify and Acknowledge

King David was great at expressing his feelings, and he didn't shy away from them. He'd make bold statements like this from Psalm 139:19–22 (CJB): "God, if only you would kill off the wicked! Men of blood, get away from me! They invoke your name for their crafty schemes; yes, your enemies misuse it. ADONAI, how I hate those who hate you! I feel such disgust with those who defy you! I hate them with unlimited hatred! They have become my enemies too."

Can you feel the intensity?

"I hate them with unlimited hatred!"

Wow. He dumps all this on God but invites Him to work out those feelings—a beautiful vulnerability that ends with this in Psalm 139:23–24 (CJB): "Examine me, God, and know my heart; test me, and know my thoughts. See if there is in me any hurtful way, and lead me along the eternal way."

King David is brutally honest with God and, in essence, says, "I have all this emotion and I don't know what to do with it. But I invite you in, Father. Process this with me and show me what to do with my feelings." He opens himself to receive from the Lord, and throughout his straightforward writings in the Psalms, he reveals how comfortable he is sharing with Him.

King David shows us we can be real, safely express our feelings to our heavenly Father, and let Him gently examine and direct us.

Becoming aware, I started with pouring out to God.

"I hate this! I feel so uncomfortable with all this 'feely' stuff. Help me to sort this out and become more at ease."

I explored my emotions with the One who created them and asked Him to search, help, and teach me what to do.

I became more aware of what I felt. Once signaled by my inner feelings, I would acknowledge them and work on identifying who it was that needed to be heard. As I leaned in to those inside, I started to see various characters trying to help me.

My first practical application in deciphering and identifying who was speaking from within was over dinner with my husband. In 2018, while working on reconnecting, we took a trip to Las Vegas where I allowed myself to explore what was happening on the inside and who was filing complaints.

David and I went to an upscale restaurant. Once seated, we were tended to straight away by the waiter, but as the evening went on, we received less and less attention until we were practically ignored.

I sensed David was growing upset, which made me anxious. At the time, I couldn't decipher *why* I felt that way. My anxiety was the first sign, so I listened to it.

In the past, I would've repressed that emotion and evoked a later feeling of disappointment because our night went amiss. Sometimes, after repressing what I felt, I'd get angry the next day and blow up at David. Slowly, I learned to embrace what I felt in each moment. When I sensed my own anxiety rise, I asked myself, *Why?*

What's going on that makes me become anxious when David gets upset? Which one of my inner personalities was vying for my attention?

Halfway through the meal, the waiter was nowhere to be found. Instead of enjoying our meal and conversation, we became short with one another. David grew more irritated, and I got more anxious—a common cycle for us.

When our server arrived, he placed the check on our table and whizzed off to his next customer without a word. He didn't even offer a "How was everything?" or "Would you like dessert?"

David had had enough and stated, "His service was terrible. I'm not leaving a tip!"

I felt a wave of heat rise to my chest. "You can't do that. You have to leave him a tip."

He put his hand up to signal me to stop. "Not now!" Anger rose inside me, but he signed the credit card receipt and said, "It'd be nice if *for once* you stood by me."

I had an arsenal of arguments for every time I've stood by him. I had so much to say, but our date night had spiraled, and I just wanted to leave. I'd participated in that argument before. It never got us out of the cycle; it just kept leading us in circles, chasing who was right. At least I'd recognized my old pattern of arguing and leaned in to a new one.

That was new territory.

After things settled, I reflected on the night, utilizing the tools I'd learned thus far.

What happened, and why did I become so uneasy when my husband got upset? Wasn't he right to be upset?

I sat with my questions, but I didn't have any answers.

Then, a memory surfaced.

I was a little girl sitting in my parent's station wagon. The motor was idling, and my mom was inside the house saying something to my dad. They emerged and argued on the front porch.

Alone in the confines of the car, I listened over the constant hum of the motor. I couldn't hear their exact words, only yelling.

I twirled a lock of hair around my finger as if it would bring some comfort to my unease as questions raced through my little mind.

Why are my mom and dad so angry? Are they separating? Will I be late for school?

Each internal question brought on more fear.

Pondering the dinner date with David and my childhood experience, I wondered if I somehow created a "little girl personality" that lived within—one who was fearful of arguing.

As I processed my new knowledge, I thought about the personalities of my feelings that developed through the years. Who were they? Could they help me or hinder me? Was one of those characters running the show the night of the dinner? I combed through a probable dialogue with the characters at my inner table that might've been at work the night in Las Vegas.

Little Girl: "Hello, everyone! I'm feeling scared here."

The Magician (who distracts me from feeling): "Little Girl, look over there. The couple at the other table is having a good time."

The Nervous Nellie (shaking and nervous): "Come on, now. Let's not get upset."

The People Pleaser: "I've got an idea. How about we find a way to appease David? Then things should settle down."

Little Girl: "None of this is working! I'm getting more frightened."

The Religious Pharisee: "Let's all repeat a prayer and cast out the golden calf of fear."

The People Pleaser: "Come on, Pharisee! We can't just break out in prayer in the middle of a restaurant. Let's get David comfortable so he chooses us and doesn't storm out of here."

The Avoider: "Can't we all just leave and go to bed? Let's deal with this tomorrow."

The Introvert: "I agree. Let's find a quiet space and throw the covers over our heads."

Little Girl: "No, we can't be alone! Remember when we were abandoned at the racetrack and how scared we were? I need to feel secure and loved!"

The Actress: "Daaa-ling, it's okay…We're not going to separate. Get yourself together, and act as if everything's fine."

Mrs. Anger: "That's it! I've had enough! The girl is scared. I'm going to yell at David for getting her upset."

The Control Freak: "Now, now, Mrs. Anger, getting upset won't work. Everyone, just give me control, and I'll fix it."

The Manager: "Order! Everyone settle down and listen up. Here's the plan…"

With that, I'd just identified my first inner workings of who was anxious within—the little girl inside. She was trying to tell me what she'd learned over the years: when someone gets angry, they leave her alone, and she feels unloved. And she desperately wanted a night of love and connection.

Identifying and acknowledging the key player that invoked my fears kept the rest of the clan from clambering for resolution in future situations. Next time, it could be any one of them that needed care: Mrs. Anger, Control Freak, or Avoider. The practice of pinpointing who caused angst helped me manage and articulate what I needed and kept me closely connected to those I loved.

After learning how to recognize the voices within and become more readily tuned into who it was that spoke at my emotional table, I discovered that I was the ultimate "manager" of my feelings, so I have the power to direct those trying to run the show. While no one person at the table got a complete say, it was important to let them speak. As such, I addressed my own unease by letting that personality know that I've got this.

Once my feelings were identified, I started owning them. I stopped apologizing for them and gave myself the space to feel truthfully. That was life changing for me.

While I'd slayed my abandonment giant and quit dragging it along, there were still scars from the battle. Those wounds, when dealt with, healed over time but were still a part of the landscape of my life. Receiving and managing them was the healthiest thing I could do.

In the future, when the little girl becomes afraid, I'll readily identify her and piece together why I'm feeling anxious. *David's upset, so I'm feeling anxious. Oh yeah, I falsely believe that if those close to me get upset, they will leave. Got it.*

After identifying her, I was free to acknowledge and tend to her by saying, "I understand you're afraid and you believe if David gets upset, he'll leave. That's what we learned so many years ago, and it's been reinforced through past experiences. But if we're left alone, I'll take care of us." I also prayed and asked God to help with my little girl fear.

I felt free to deal with conversations with David in a productive manner and not let my fear of abandonment take over. I also realized that David had his own inner personalities that sat around his table. Knowing more about what circled him helped me respond better to a situation that respected his view of the world and those that lived inside him.

If we should ever be in a position like that again, I know how to calm the little girl who gets anxious. I know I'm able to agree or disagree with David in a healthy manner.

So, this is how I see the conversation going:

"His service was terrible. I'm not leaving a tip!"

I feel heat rise in my chest. "I agree; his service was terrible."

Or, "While his service was not great, I'd like you to still leave a tip. But it's your decision."

Giving David a choice allows me to stay connected to him and not let my fear rule. The manager in me can make solid decisions.

***

Feelings—those that sit around the inner internal table—are to be honored, heard, and respected. While they don't get a complete say, they're saying something important.

If someone asks me a question that requires a vulnerable answer, they might've struck a nerve with "The Actress" in me. She's the one afraid to be vulnerable because she might get hurt. Perhaps her warning is valid; after all, she's trying to protect me. Still, as the manager, I assess the risk and proceed from there. I don't let my feelings of being hurt rule, but I get to decide whether I should share my vulnerability in a conversation and if that person is a safe space. I'll also ask God for wisdom.

There are other voices that need to be dealt with. Satan's voice sounds the most frightening, but he only has the power that I allow him to have. When I hear Satan's voice, it's one of condemnation and accusation. Scripture says he's "the accuser of our brothers and sisters" (Revelation 12:10 [NIV]). His dark whispers say things like, "You're trapped as a little girl, and no one will rescue you," and, "You never stand by David. You're a bad wife."

I've identified those demeaning words and renounced them—I receive *not*.

God's voice, on the other hand, is the most powerful and the one to listen closely to and receive all He has to say. For me, it comes in the form of a thought dropped into my mind that I wouldn't typically think about or a whisper that says things differently than I do. Scripture says, "For my thoughts are not your thoughts, neither are your ways my ways" (Isaiah 55:8 [NIV]). God gently directs, corrects, advises, and praises, and those thoughts and whispers are the ones I know to be His.

God says things like:

"I've got you. You are okay."

"Don't go that way, let's go this way."

"I will never leave you nor forsake you."

"I have a better plan."

"Trust me."

"You are complete in me."

"You are beautiful, and you are mine."

Knowing the difference between the destroyer's voice and God's voice allows me to *receive not* Satan's destructive words and *receive* my Father's truth. Once I know the voice I should follow, I can work on my own inner voices and ask God for help, direction, and wisdom.

After identifying those around my inner table, it was time to decipher and articulate them.

Decipher

There's a story about a blind beggar named Bartimaeus in Mark 10:46–52 (CJB). He was sitting by the side of the road, and as a large crowd passed by, he heard that Jesus was in the crowd. He began shouting, "Yeshua! Son of David! Have pity on me!" Many people scolded him and told him to be quiet, but he shouted even louder, "Son of David, have pity on me!"

My curiosity perked up. *What did he know about Jesus? And why did he believe that Jesus could help him?*

"When he heard it was Yeshua from Nazareth, he started shouting" (Mark 10:47 [CJB]).

Ah, he knew of Jesus. Had he heard of His miracles?

But the story felt like it was about more than simply hearing of Jesus. The blind man started shouting. There were more than rumors or stories about Jesus's power; there seemed to be something that moved him.

Squinting as if he could see through blind eyes, I felt the longing and desperation Bartimaeus must've experienced. As Jesus passed by, was he overcome by a deep knowing that Jesus is the true and living God?

This was his chance to receive from God, and he wasn't going to let anyone or anything come between him and Jesus. He wouldn't allow Jesus to pass by without His healing and blessing.

Despite the hushing from the crowd, the dismissed beggar grew more eager. He knew he was in the presence of the Holy One, and his soul cried out from the deepest place—so much so that his cry stopped Jesus in His tracks.

"Yeshua stopped and said, 'Call him over!' They called to the blind man, 'Courage! Get up! He's calling for you!' Throwing down his blanket, he jumped up and came over to Yeshua. 'What do you want me to do for you?' asked Yeshua. The blind man said to him, 'Rabbi, let me be able to see again.' Yeshua said to him, 'Go! Your trust has healed you.' Instantly he received his sight and followed him on the road" (Mark 10:49–52 [CJB]).

One sentence stirred inside me, and I didn't know why. I sat propped up on my bed and wrote the following words in my journal: "What do you want me to do for you?" I drew circles around the statement. *What if Jesus passed by me and I had one ask of Him? Would I know what I wanted?*

It seemed an easy ask for the blind man—he was blind and wanted his sight back.

But I think there was something deeper there. It was about more than his physical eyesight; Bartimaeus wanted to see spiritually too. As if to say, "Lord, let me see the unseen things." I believe he received both his physical and spiritual eyesight that day and followed Jesus on the road of life.

I pondered my own hesitations. Was I able to, in that moment, clearly articulate my deepest desires? Did I truly know what I needed? I began deciphering what I wanted and pictured Jesus saying, "Call her over."

The crowd cheered me on. "Courage! Get up! He's calling for you!"

I got to share my heart's desire with my Lord. "Rabbi, I long for reconciliation."

"Go! Your trust has healed you." Instantly, I received reconnection with my husband and followed Jesus on the road of life.

At the dinner in Las Vegas, how would my night have gone if I was able to identify the feelings that were acting up and decipher what I needed?

After identifying the little girl's fear, the next step was to understand what I needed in the moment. I might've asked myself, "What do I need to feel okay when David is upset?" By pinpointing the need, I could then articulate it to myself, to God, and to David.

Articulate

Stating what I felt and what I needed, even if to myself, was difficult for me. It felt vulnerable and needy. However, doing so was actually empowering. I came to understand that if I shared my feelings and asked for help, I'd still be able to tend to myself if that person couldn't help me. I didn't need anyone's help, but it was a bonus if they could.

I learned to get more comfortable stating my needs because I was free to know that it wasn't up to David, my mom, or my friends to make me feel okay; it was up to me. With that freedom, I'm confident to share.

I've since learned that someone can't tell me how I *should* feel. My feelings are valid, and I have a right to them.

That doesn't mean I should wallow, but I need to honor them and give them their proper space. Acknowledging them allowed me to recognize whose voice led the conversation around the table and what the true message was. Then, I could decipher my needs and articulate them.

I wanted to be more like Bartimaeus—knowing exactly what I needed and stating it.

It was difficult in the beginning. I only managed to express a few simple words, and even that was a struggle. It was unusual for me to say those things out loud, so I opted to name them quietly. I started with a whisper of "I feel scared," "I feel uncertain," and "I feel sad."

Once I started identifying my emotions, I was able to name more: joyful, suspicious, angry, perplexed, overwhelmed, anxious, fearful, teary, jealous, disconnected, mistrusting, lonely, dismissed, hurt, unheard, hopeful. I was becoming un-numb and beginning to come to life, perhaps for the first time ever.

As I got better at articulating my feelings, I worked on articulating what I needed: "I'm feeling vulnerable." So, I'd ask myself, "Okay, what do you need?" And I'd respond, "I need to feel safe in this conversation." Next, I articulated to others, "I'm feeling vulnerable. Please remind me that I'm safe with you."

Stating what I needed to others gave them the opportunity to receive the gift of serving. If they couldn't help for whatever reason, I could care for my own needs.

I thought about being at the restaurant with David. How would the conversation go for me in the future? How could I articulate most skillfully, keep my own integrity, and be the best version of me?

"His service was terrible. I'm not leaving a tip!"

"I agree, his service was terrible, and you have every right to be upset with the waiter. As you know, my little girl within gets anxious when you're upset. The old me would want you to leave a tip and move on so we can continue our date night. But I know that's not healthy for you because you'd be silently brooding on it—which isn't good for us. Leave a tip or not, you do what's right for you. I'll work on calming myself. Could you just tell me that once we leave together, we won't let this ruin the rest of our night, and we can continue to have a good time?"

Once I began changing what I could—welcoming and listening to those feelings that encircled my inner table, deciphering what I needed, and articulating to others—I became free to receive me and those I loved. I became my own hero, caring for my own wounds and letting David in so he could tend to my scars too.

David was learning to lovingly stand toe-to-toe with me. He learned that helping me go through my emotional baggage wasn't always healthy for him if it came at the expense of his own integrity. He began to say things like, "I've got you; you're okay—we're okay, but I'm upset with the waiter, so I'm not going to leave a tip."

Our dynamic was changing for the better. We'd still catch ourselves falling into old habits, like fighting in unproductive circles, but we took notice and stopped.

We were learning to receive.

Can you name those who sit around your table? Can you hear them calling out to be heard and acknowledged? Are you willing to listen, reassure, and care for them? Each one is telling you something. Each voice provides important warnings and messages so you can be the healthiest version of you. But remember, only you—as the manager—get the final say. Then, you can decipher your needs and clearly articulate them. This releases you to receive from God, from yourself, and from others. This frees you to receive.

15

Practice Five –
Opening and Closing

With cheerful expectancy,
knowing what you ask is granted
to the extent I'm open to receive!
—Russell Dennis

I LISTENED TO A BRIAN BUFFINI PODCAST INTERVIEW WITH GUEST Alison Levine,[16] who's ascended the highest peaks on every continent and climbed Mount Everest twice. In her first attempt, she got within two hundred feet of the summit, but a storm stopped her from reaching the top, so she was forced to turn back. She must've felt defeated after being that close.

While Alison was honest about her disappointment, she also said, "Most people think the summit is the goal when in actuality, the summit is only the halfway point. You still have to get down the mountain alive." So, she made her way down the mountain and lived to climb another day.

She continued. "It's not a straight line to get to the top of Mount Everest."

---

16. Brian Buffini, Interview with Alison Levine, *What's Your Everest*, podcast audio, March 28, 2017, https://www.thebrianbuffinishow.com/whats-everest-043/.

I was surprised at her statement because I'd always imagined the climb as a straight ascent. Alison explained how everyone assumed they'd just climb from their base camp.

She said it took ten days of hiking just to reach her base camp, and once there, she rested and let her body acclimate to the altitude before heading up to camp one.

She shared how the journey up is a series of climbs and descents. When leaving camp one, she climbed to camp two, then descended back to camp one. The body can then adjust to the altitude before continuing to climb back up to camp two. After some rest, she climbed to camp three, back down to two, then back up to three. Alison explained that there were several parts of the mountain that she climbed more than once.

She talked about the emotional toll of reaching each higher level, then having to come back down the mountain to the previous camp. She said it messed with your mind, so I paused the podcast to ponder that immense thought.

I've never physically climbed a mountain, but I've emotionally hiked one. After trekking through a decade of desert season—ten years of financially leading and emotionally trying to help David—I was surprised to find I was only at the base camp of my mountain.

Discovering we came out of that decade wounded and disconnected, I was asked to climb a mountain of reconciliation, but I felt too exhausted.

How often did I falsely believe that life should be a direct path or a linear ascent to my destination? What if the trek was intended to be asymmetrical? What if our souls needed to climb back down to a lower level before ascending to adjust to the altitude of the fallen world?

I pressed play and resumed the podcast.

Alison explained that on the mountain, as in life, we need to go back down to the previous camp to not only allow the body time to acclimate but also prepare the mind for what's to come. We need to be emotionally ready and fortify the mind to reach the summit and get back *down* the mountain alive. And then came her profound statement:

"Backing up is not the same as backing down."

Alison explained that in climbing a mountain, you must descend first to climb up farther. She never backed down, but she had to back up several times to make it to the top. In 2010, on her second attempt, Alison finally made it to the summit of Mount Everest.

How many times had I felt discouraged and tired from climbing? I would've never made it if God hadn't given me the grace to stop along the way and send me back to the lower camp before climbing farther. I learned to give myself time to stop and process my own journey, drop the weight of things that weren't meant to be carried, and retreat to the previous camp to truly prepare myself for the next ascent. I'd backed up, but not backed down. For that, I was proud.

It was in those restful moments at base camp where I learned to receive. I discovered how to open my heart to God's goodness and close it to all things that weren't from Him. I found a way to receive *me* and love who I am.

I thought about how Moses ascended Mount Sinai many times to meet with God. There are two things we tend to remember about that story. When Moses received the Ten Commandments and went down to share with his people, reaching the summit was only part of the journey. He needed to get back down the mountain in order to bring the message to the Israelites. So, God's glory shone on Moses.

But when he got to the base of Mount Sinai, he discovered the Israelites had turned from God. In the short time he was on the mountain, his own people had turned to a false god—worshipping a golden calf. Moses was so upset that he broke the stone tablets.

So, Moses ascended the mountain again to get a second copy. "Chisel out two stone tablets like the first ones, and I will write on them the words that were on the first tablets, which you broke" (Exodus 34:1 [NIV]).

I tend to think of this ascent as Moses's second climb, but it was actually his eighth![17]

Moses's various climbs reminded me of Alison's and her tablets of truth—lessons she carried home with her.

I'm descending my own mountain now. I've received, but I need to do something with what's been given to me. Tucked under my arm are the "tablets" with the message God has shown me—the writing of what I've discovered—first for me, then to share with others.

Through this journey, I learned transformational processes. In descending the mountain, I slowly began opening my heart to God's goodness and, when needed, closing it to the things that aren't of God. Further opening my heart and truly receiving came through an unusual way: a friend's response to a text.

Attitude, Believe, Open

I'd sent an encouraging message to a friend named Russell Dennis. His response lingered with me so much so that I read it over and over again.

He said, "With cheerful expectancy, knowing what you ask is granted to the extent I'm open to receive!"

Russell was cheerful and had a joyful attitude over the blessing of my encouragement. He read my message with expectancy,

---

17. "How Many Times Did Moses Ascend Mount Sinai?" Got Questions, accessed January 25, 2022, https://www.gotquestions.org/Moses-on-Mount-Sinai.html.

claimed it, and believed it was granted to him. Initially, he was open to receive whatever God might say through me, but there was a portion of the promise that was up to him: he had to open himself up more to completely receive. I paused at the wisdom of his words. How had I prevented my ability to receive because I hadn't been fully open? The action of opening my heart was something I willfully had to do. I was intrigued and needed to break down the message.

The Attitude of the Heart

I considered Russell's posture toward my message. To truly receive, I must begin with a positive attitude. I thought about all the times I'd unintentionally closed myself off to receiving a message because my heart eroded as life played out in harsh realities. Life wears out childlike expectancy, joy becomes jaded, and life's assaults beat down cheerfulness.

Except the transformation I experienced on my emotional mountain taught me that happiness is my choice. I learned how to better care for my own heart and trust myself to open or close it when needed. But the truth remained—there were times I felt discouraged and joy-sapped. How many precious words hadn't made their way through because I wouldn't open up to them?

Looking back on my trek, my posture changed from skeptic and the utter distrust of others (including myself) to trusting my own inner wisdom and God's Holy Spirit.

I learned anew how to better guard my heart and let my "inner guide" alert and lead me down the right path. And for that, I was hopeful and chose cheerful expectancy.

I took hold of what it meant to receive and not receive. The trek taught me how to healthily guard my heart, which reminded me of Proverbs 4:23 (NIV).

"Above all else, guard your heart, for everything you do flows from it."

I read the scripture from the Complete Jewish Bible to get a different perspective.

"Above everything else, guard your heart; for it is the source of life's consequences. Keep crooked speech out of your mouth, banish deceit from your lips. Let your eyes look straight ahead, fix your gaze on what lies in front of you. Level the path for your feet, let all your ways be properly prepared; then deviate neither right nor left; and keep your foot far from evil" (Proverbs 4:23–27 [CJB]).

The scripture doesn't say build a wall around your heart; it says to guard it. Guard in Hebrew means "keeper, watchman." Rather than hide behind walls to follow the scripture's guidance, we're instructed to be keepers of the heart and rule over it.

To be a watchman or watchwoman of our hearts is actually an offensive play. The heart is the source of life's consequences, so we must proactively defend it from becoming jaded or skeptical. That's how we continue to live with expectancy—by guarding what comes in and out, we're rulers of our own hearts.

I'm the only one who can keep myself safe (with God's directive). So, I can open my heart with expectancy to receive because I trust my inner guide. God's Spirit will signal the watchwoman in me if something shouldn't be received. I trust the process, so I can state like Russell, "With cheerful expectancy," I will be open to receive.

Believe by Knowing What You Ask For is Granted

Once I began trusting myself to be the watchwoman who confidently opened and closed my own heart, I was steady enough to receive and believe. By believing in myself and knowing God was my guide, I grew stronger in my faith and completely opened my heart. When opening to a blessing, I stated faithfully, "I believe what you ask for is granted."

I had a coffee meeting with someone I hardly knew. In our discussion, the person said to me, "You're a hero." Immediately, I wanted to reject the statement. I was embarrassed. Besides, they didn't *know* me, so how could they say I'm a hero? But I pushed back the embarrassment to avoid rejecting the word being given.

Receiving a compliment wasn't easy for me. Usually, I'd laugh or make a joke to brush it off. That time, I pressed myself to stay in the discomfort and graciously accept it, even if I had to squirm through it.

I thought for certain the person was angling about the open house attack and was going to compliment my bravery. The word "hero" made me uncomfortable because it should be saved for those serving in our military and our police officers, doctors, and nurses.

"I'm not sure what you mean," I responded.

"Well, I'm reading this book, and it defines a hero as 'someone who pours a little bit of themselves into you, leaving you better than they found you.'[18] Even though we don't know each other well, I've gotten to know you a little. And today, you poured some of yourself into me and made me better."

With joyful expectancy, I listened, processed without sarcasm

____

18. Kevin Brown, *The Hero Effect: Being Your Best When It Matters Most* (2017), 17.

or deflection, and let it linger. I then realized I'd been given a gift of words I should humbly receive. It didn't matter if I believed I was a hero or not or what my own definition of a hero was. What that person said was their experience of me, and I needed to open to them.

"That's very kind of you. Thank you," I replied.

I thought about Russell's response. "Knowing that what you ask for (or say) is granted." Those sweet words couldn't manifest themselves in my life if I didn't grant them permission to come in. So, I opened the door to my heart and let the word "hero" enter.

In the conversation, I listened well, not trying to fix any problems, and simply asked questions. Because of that, the person felt love and acceptance. They left feeling better than when they showed up. When the time came for them to pour into me by calling me a hero, I had a choice: receive or reject. I chose to believe and receive. *What you say is granted into my heart.*

Equally important is the ability to unemotionally receive productive criticism from someone trusted. In receiving, I ask myself, *Is this true? Is this a healthy assessment? And should I receive or reject it?* Being honest with myself allows me to receive things I might not want to hear. I assess within if pride has stopped me from receiving. If so, I block pride so I can be open to the words I don't want to hear.

That's the power of discovering the true me. I'm trusting the watchwoman of my heart (instructed by God's Spirit), believing she'll show me what to open and close to.

It's not only building my faith; it forces me to live out faith. Believe and receive.

Opening to the Extent I'm Open to Receive

The final words Russell used caught my attention. "To the extent I'm open to receive."

He was aware that, at times, he wasn't completely open, and perhaps in certain situations, he closed himself off. Interestingly, even though Russell had cheerful expectancy and the faith to believe the word spoken was granted, he still had to open himself up *more fully* to receive.

Acts 20:35 (NIV) says, "Remembering the words the Lord Jesus himself said: 'It is more blessed to give than to receive.'"

The Complete Jewish Bible interprets it another way: "There is more happiness in giving than in receiving" (Acts 20:35).

It's more blessed, holy, and consecrated—there's more happiness in giving. God wants our hearts to be free from greed and holding onto things. So, it's good to give and bless others, but there needs to be a receiver—someone on the other end who's open to receive.

Even though it's better to give, it's *harder* to receive. Receiving doesn't come naturally and takes humble practice. It's very difficult for me to receive something from another person. When I do, I realize that I plot and plan what I can do to return the favor before I even say thank you. The world spins on the axis of quid pro quo. If I receive something from you, I need to exchange something of value for what you've given me.

I was at a party, and a friend introduced me to someone. She said, "Dawna is writing a book. She's also the founder of a growing network of women called 'Jericho Girls.'" I felt embarrassed and noticed my mind was searching for the best way to downplay my friend's words or deflect by sharing my friend's accomplishments too.

Instead, I fought off my feelings, calmed my mind, and remained silent. When my friend, Shannon, finished speaking, I simply thanked her. Then the other person asked me questions, which led to a good conversation.

There are many occasions where I deflect goodness, and I know I'm not alone. I've heard others divert too:

"You are a great mom."
Response: "You haven't seen me interact with my kiddos at
home."

"I bought this for you."
Reply: "Oh, you shouldn't have. I feel bad that I didn't get you
anything."

"Dude, you're so handsome."
Comeback: "You need glasses."

Receiving is the classroom of humility. And with practice, it gets easier.

Whether an actual gift, a compliment, a word of truth, or some advice, I simply pause, take in the moment, open my heart, and say thank you.

Luke 6:35 teaches that not everything in life is a transaction. "Do good, and lend, expecting nothing in return." In other words, give, and don't expect anything back. Receive and don't feel like you have to reciprocate. In giving, I'm loosening my grip on worldly things. In receiving, I'm training to combat pride.

The best example is the gift of salvation. God's gift of eternity is free, and He doesn't require me to give Him anything in return. The act of receiving without reciprocating frees my heart to humbly know Him and His good gifts. There's nothing to do except joyfully receive salvation, believe that Jesus is the Son of God—the Messiah—then invite Him into my heart to lead my life. All that's required is to open my heart and receive Him.

God made receiving uncomplicated—open your heart and invite Him in. While it seems straightforward, some of us wrestle with the fact that God made it so easy. I feel like I should perform a bunch of righteous acts to reciprocate his free gift of love. Shouldn't I have to jump through hoops to repay what he's offered?

Receiving should be easy, but it's not because we've complicated it. We tend to insert our own ideas and agendas and measure our own worth before receiving, if we even receive at all. And telling myself, "Just do it, Dawna. Simply open your heart," doesn't happen instantly; I have to work on it.

I continue practicing the art of opening to this day. I'm still imperfectly struggling with it, but I've employed some simple tactics that help in the process. One way to implement the practice of opening the heart and receiving came from my best friend, Julieann, who I've nicknamed Buddy. It was simple and fun.

The night before speaking at a conference, I needed to write some thank you notes for all who helped put the program together. I was so tired and needed sleep, but I didn't want to do it in the morning, so I had to get it done that night. Buddy volunteered to help me write the notes. As fatigue set in, we became giddy. She said to me, "Have you seen Jimmy Fallon on *The Tonight Show* do his skit writing thank you notes?"

"I think so, but remind me."

"Jimmy does a skit where he writes thank you notes. He cues music and, in dramatic fashion, writes thank you notes for very silly things."

Before I could respond, Buddy said, "Cue the music." She lifted her hand and pretended to write the thank you note in the air. "Dear

Sharron, thank you…" Buddy emphasized the *th* and drew out the word *you*. It sounded like *tttttthhhhank YOU!* We laughed so hard we cried. It took even longer to get the thank you notes done because we kept mimicking Jimmy Fallon as we wrote each one.

I began teaching the ladies in my inner circle how to receive by using that example. I told them when receiving a compliment, imagine cueing the music and writing a "thank you note" in the air. That prepares the heart in a joyful, cheerful, and silly way to receive just about anything. It also primes the heart to believe and receive all that you know to be good for you because receiving or receiving not is generous to the soul.

Opening is a willful practice done under the supervision of my inner wisdom—God's Holy Spirit that directs and guides me. I changed my attitude and became expectant. I developed a new-found confidence, understanding I could trust myself to guard my own heart and believe in the watchwoman who chose to open the gates of her heart or shut them.

I developed my faith and believed in God, who led me where I needed to go. I knew I could trust Him to tell me when to open and when to close my heart. Believing begins by trusting yourself to be a good steward of what to open and close to and honing the belief that God will guide you as you embark on the process.

Then I took it one step at a time, opening to the extent I felt comfortable with at each moment, and continued to practice and train my heart to open and close.

It's a lifelong practice that'll continue to shape my soul and keep it humble. I continually practice receiving and write "thank you notes" in the air. Like Russell, I grew to say, "With cheerful expectancy, knowing what you ask for is granted to the extent I'm open to receive!"

16

Practice Six – The Breathable List

Every man has his mountain.
I'm carving mine.
—Korczak Ziółkowski

I WAS LOOKING DEEPLY AT MY WILLINGNESS TO ACCEPT OR REJECT — to receive and receive not. Having a cheerful attitude, believing in faith, and opening to the truest version of myself was a free-will choice and daily decision.

Some days were easier than others, but I kept working on bettering myself. There were two truths I knew for certain:

1. I didn't like the feeling of discomfort. Change was uncomfortable, so it seemed safer to stay in old, familiar, and dysfunctional habits.

2. I was free to choose complacency or transformation—and I knew that, ultimately, transformation freed me.

I'd experienced the power that comes from leaving unproductive patterns. It was my motivation to continually press myself. Real freedom and empowerment derived from stepping away from the old and embracing the new.

Thus far, I'd worked on my mind—taking thoughts captive and only allowing what was good, right, and true to flow. I tuned in to my intuition and dropped the weight of burdens I shouldn't carry, allowing positive things to trickle into my heart. I checked my heart's motivation, listened and honored those around my table, and implemented opening and closing my heart. Next came two practices that helped my soul. The first was making a list of what to accept and what to release.

I asked myself, *What's healthy or not for my soul right now, and what do I know to be true?*

As I lived in the moments of my life, I took each situation that presented itself and added to my list. I often subtracted things from it too. The more I learned about God, the more I realized He didn't operate using checklists. Our creative and timeless Father dwelled in the delight of the unknown. Taking inventory, I realized it was impossible to have a complete list that directed every future decision. Then, I realized I didn't need one; I just needed to ask God to show me.

I still made one, though, because that's the way I remember where I came from and where I'm headed. It wasn't comprehensive, rather one that I used as a reminder, like leaving breadcrumbs on the road in case I lost my way.

As circumstances revealed themselves or as I changed, I approached my notations with the understanding that life isn't stagnant. What I might receive or reject may be different today than it will be tomorrow. And what my values guide me to accept or reject will be different from someone else's. Nothing is forever and always—except God.

There were definitely some things that remained certain, so I quit trying to make an exhaustive one and created a "breathable list" from my journey.

My Breathable List

Receive your intuition and the peace it brings by trusting it. Reject all manufactured worry and anxiety—different from true fear.

Receive positive truths about yourself, *and* receive the things you know to be true but don't want to face. Open up to productive criticism from a trusted source, and reject any untruths about yourself that you know are false.

Receive help. Reject overbearing.

Receive the right motivations of your heart. Identify, block, and alter the unhealthy ones hidden within.

Receive your feelings and honor them. Reject their attempt to run the show.

Receive confidence and a healthy sense of self. Reject arrogance and pride.

Receive God's direction, love, and salvation. Reject Satan's deceit.

Receive grief and loss. There's a place for it in life—a season for everything. Reject anyone or anything that tries to rush the process. Your time will come to dance again.

Receive and respect triggers. Reject, slay, and quit dragging along the giants that taunt you.

Receive kindness. Reject maliciousness.

Receive deep laughter. Reject the thieves of joy.

Receive your journey. Reject thoughts of speeding it up. Complete transformation doesn't come quickly.

Receive healthy relationships and self-love. Reject *all* types of abuse, manipulation, and guilt trips.

Receive steadfastness. Reject waffling and wavering.

Receive your giftings. Reject all things that don't align.

Receive your own inner watchman/watchwoman. Reject anyone or anything that brings a deep sense of mistrust.

Receive compliments. Reject insults.

Receive change. Reject stagnancy and complacency.

Receive acceptance of yourself and the gift to just be you truthfully. Reject conforming.

Receive grace—especially to oneself. Reject self-sabotage.

Receive faithfulness. Be the person of integrity you want to be. Reject disloyalty.

Receive plentifulness. Reject gluttony.

Receive and make room for God's judgment. Reject hate and revenge.

Receive what God has given you. Reject envy and jealousy.

Receive doing your part as best as you can. Reject the illusion of control.

Receive healthy desire. Reject lust.

Receive your journey. Reject trekking without God.

Each receive and reject helped me through my daily life and difficult times. With all that in mind, there were things I hadn't lived through yet and more that led me to say, "Oh yes, receive that, Dawna," or "I hadn't thought of not accepting *that*." Certainly, there'd be many more that I'd experience in my lifetime and plenty more in the future that I'd need to write down. That's why the list should always be breathable and ready for rewrites.

Perhaps there are specific things in front of you that you need to accept or release:

- The diagnosis, or perhaps rejecting it for a second opinion. Or accepting the prognosis and the path to treatment.

- Maybe it's the simple act of saying no to the workload and yes to playing with the kiddos, spending the evening with your spouse, or talking to a friend.

- Could it be accepting the promotion or letting go of it?

- It might be listening to the investment opportunity or walking away from it.

- Is it receiving the reconciliation or accepting the breakup?

What others can you think of?

Discovering More Meaning

My season of loss was also a season of gain. As difficult as it was for me to cross a dry desert for ten years then climb a mountain, by my descent, I realized I'd changed. It seemed I'd get down the mountain alive, and that was when I got a glimpse of the true me. I was shining with the glory of God.

During my dreaded season, I complained, cried, and came against all that I didn't want to face. But through it, I actually stood firm in my faith. I loved the new version of me who transformed throughout my journey of self-discovery. I even moved closer to God than I'd ever been before.

I've always believed that our experiences have a bigger purpose and meaning than we can see or comprehend at first. As I descended my emotional mountain, I saw a bigger purpose—I'd been placed on that path to discover a better version of myself.

My hope was that I handled that season of my life well and it was pleasing to God. I also prayed my story could light someone else's painful path and remind them that *their pain wasn't in vain.*

Perhaps I'd been training for that specific moment my entire life. All I knew was as I drew closer to returning to base camp, I was starting to see that it was all worth it. I had a sense of accomplishment I didn't have before. My own words to David sealed the message that made its way into my soul.

I'd been praying vigilantly for David to become a solidified day trader. "God, he's worked so hard. Help him! Be with him, and let him achieve the success he's worked so hard for. Help David to lead again. Help him to have Your favor in his trading. He deserves it."

David had finished his trading day and came to chat with me. He told me about the events of the day and some of the good trades he made. He seemed content with his decisions, and he was "green."

I looked at him and said, "You've come a long way. It's been a learning curve, but you have overcome." And then, seemingly out of nowhere, a word of truth that I hadn't planned came about. God spoke directly through me, *and to me*, as I said, "But more than being profitable, it's who you're *becoming* in the process. You've grown in patience, maturity, and wisdom. That's more important than any profitable trade. And isn't that why we're really here? To become who we're supposed to be?"

Sure, trading and becoming the businessman David wanted to be was important, but not as important as attaining his highest calling—a steadfast man of God.

I realized the same held true for me. My decade of loss was a season of gain. It was meant for me to travel and shape me into who God created me to be. My pain wasn't in vain. I hated the journey but loved the person I became because of it.

While I often questioned, *Isn't there an easier way?* Walking the hard road created smooth edges. There is always a broader picture. Each of us must become the best versions of ourselves to fulfill the unique calling we have for our lives. No matter what we do, the utmost goal is transformation. God leads us to live the best versions of ourselves—the way he ultimately created us to be.

I thought about Alison's words from the podcast interview. She said she imagined that standing on the summit of Mount Everest would be this amazing moment—and it was—but there was something more profound than making it to the peak and standing on it.

Her awe came from not just reaching the top of Mount Everest but in the discovery of who she'd become in the ascent and descent—a relentless woman who never gave up.

I looked back and felt extreme thankfulness for who I'd become through my own journey. I really admired myself for staggering through the desert, making the climb up my mountain, and getting back to base camp alive. I'd discovered how to receive all of me, and I found ways I needed to tweak my character and strengthen the gifts that were already there. Yes, there was much more to the desert season and mountain trek.

The summit is not our end goal. The summit is only the halfway point. We still have to get down the mountain alive, each of us in our own way and in our own time.

"Backing up is not the same as backing down."

I thought about how Alison encouraged us to keep our minds right—not allowing the setbacks or having to retrace steps take an emotional toll. There was a purpose for going back down the mountain before ascending farther.

She also said there was a part of the mountain called the Khumbu Glacier where ice glaciers measured up to the size of apartment buildings. As temperatures warmed up, the ice glaciers started to move and would sometimes break and fall. While traversing those open areas on the mountain, she learned you couldn't become complacent.

"Complacency will kill you. You have to keep moving and stay alert."

Each of us are called to climb. Some are faced with hills, and others have fourteeners. Sometimes, we're called to climb Everest. Whatever the journey entails, we need to be mindful of who we grow into during the process. We mustn't become complacent, and we have to make it back down alive.

At some point in our lives, all of us will reach a crevasse. We climb over the deep cracks of life's fractures. Some are deeper, and some are wider, but we face them in various forms. Will we survive them? Who do we become in the process? We fulfill the purposes of God and become our trustiest selves by facing our mountains.

As we climb our individual mountains, we can choose to carve something beautiful.

Perhaps if I would've understood that my climb was shaping me for the better and fulfilling eternal purposes, maybe—just maybe—I would've faced my season with hope and optimism.

Receiving means opening to the peace and purposes of God completely and closing to the darkness of the world.

Making a breathable list to add to has made me a better watchwoman over my soul. It's been a written reminder of my path and how far I've come. It's also a guide to remind me what to be open to and what not to let in. And it led me to my final soul-shaping practice—to receive my journey.

17

Practice Seven – Acceptance

I could still play tennis,
but I needed to resort to a different style of play.
— Bill Clarke

IN 1991, I WITNESSED THE MOST BEAUTIFUL DISPLAY OF ACCEPtance. My mother-in-law, Caryl, lost her daddy. His name was Charles Oswald Rowe. His friends called him Ozzie, and we called him Papa. Papa was the kindest man I'd ever met. His deep blue eyes transported me to the throne room of God. We said our goodbyes on a hillside in the West San Fernando Valley in California when it was his time to go home and be with God.

Caryl had barely processed the loss of her father when, just two weeks later, her husband, Dave, died suddenly of a heart attack at the age of fifty-three. Stripped of her partner, the shock and awe of Dave's death left a traumatic hole in Caryl's heart. It left scars for all of us—David, his brother, and me.

Caryl was heartbroken. She lost the two most important men in her life a mere two weeks apart. Dazed and confused, she pressed on. In the days that followed, I watched her closely and saw something profoundly beautiful about her. Subtly, she wore a supernatural strength. Somehow buried in her grief-filled heart was a level of trust I'd never seen or experienced.

Instead of entering into their "golden years," she was trusting God's plan of "retirement." Rather than boarding a plane hand-in-hand for their upcoming trip to Spain, she was stepping into an unplanned journey of widowhood.

I watched her praise God for her husband's safe trip "home." Even in shock, when Dave suddenly died, Caryl clung to trusting God and believed in His purpose to call Dave to his heavenly home.

It was sad and beautiful at the same time.

As I observed Caryl, I learned something very profound—how to continually trust God. By trusting Him, it brought about peaceful acceptance.

Trusting and Thanking

Acceptance begins with trust. I don't have to like my circumstances, but I must consider there's a bigger picture and more to what's physically seen. I have to believe in someone unimaginably wiser, stronger, and omniscient. If I don't, then what's the meaning of life's assaults? Somehow, my soul knows there's a greater purpose to the landslides and that God is in control of them.

The numerous avalanches I faced during my mountain climb sent me tumbling, and I found myself suffocating under the weight of it all. Some were caused by human choice, others seemed like God triggered them. After attempting to catch myself time and time again, I became weary.

I wouldn't allow myself to believe that the disconnect could've taken place, especially after a very long season of hard work, living well, and believing that David and I were unbreakable. I wouldn't accept my reality or pain, and it felt oddly safe in the arms of denial.

Eventually, I began to doubt God's goodness and debated the meaning of the challenges. I questioned the truths I once held so dear.

In my searching, I asked:

How could God allow this to happen?

Did God really say He'd protect you?

How can there be meaning or purpose in this?

I became untrusting of God, myself, and others.

One day, I felt a glimmer of strength, but it felt like it would disappear in an instant. In that moment, I acted on my fleeting strength to crack open my Bible in search of some resemblance—any resemblance—of the trust in God I once had. So, I opened and read Psalm 62:8–9 (CJB).

"My safety and honor rest on God. My strong rock and refuge are in God. Trust in him, people, at all times; pour out your heart before him; God is a refuge for us."

I thought about the words on the page.

My safety rests on God. Where had God been in all this?

Instead of allowing these questions into my heart and soul, I first took them to God.

"I need to talk to you about this, Lord," I said.

I shared my heartache and disappointments. With a whisper, I said, "Help me trust You again, Lord."

It simply began there. Another three-year journey was ahead of me, and it wasn't easy. From 2017 to 2020, I faced the hard things: everything that had gone wrong, all the wasted years, and my part in it.

Trust began with remembering there is a purpose to suffering. Even when I doubted, the deep-rooted belief that there's more to this life lingered deep within, and I couldn't escape it. Even though it felt like God checked out, He was still there in the recesses of my soul. Perhaps He hadn't left but made Himself less known to let me discover what I'm really capable of.

Steadily, I regained footing. And the more I read His word and deeply shared with Him, I felt my trust in God return. Late in 2020, I felt a shift. Rather than allowing distrust and denial to ask *me* questions and make room for doubt, I continually took my questions to God and unknowingly made room in my heart for acceptance.

Peace came from opening my heart and trusting Him unwaveringly, receiving all that God has ordained, even in extreme seasons of disappointment, hurt, and the finality of loss that life certainly delivers.

As the days turned into months, I felt my heart trust in myself and others once again too.

"And without **trusting**, it is impossible to be well pleasing to God" (Hebrews 11:6 [CJB]).

Well pleasing—I wanted that. I longed to be well pleasing to God. So, I pressed forward.

One morning while reading scripture, His voice came to me in the form of a thought.

"Allow yourself to be thankful," He said.

"Thankful? How in the world do you want me to feel gratitude for this journey?"

Silence. I reread the passage.

"Rejoice always, pray continually, give thanks in all circumstances; for this is God's will for you in Christ Jesus" (1 Thessalonians 5:16–18 [NIV]).

Suddenly, I could see.

Acceptance doesn't mean you receive everything that comes to you. We give thanks *in* all circumstances, but we don't have to give thanks *for* all circumstances.

Do you see the difference?

I hated the journey, and I wasn't thankful for it, but I still thanked God *in* it.

Acceptance meant learning to receive all and give thanks to God *in* it and through it. And that's when I began the process of acceptance—an unhurried pace of looking at difficult things and asking myself how I would do it differently moving forward. I knew I needed to trust God and be thankful for my transformation *while in* hard places.

I felt hopeful.

"Trust in the Lord with all your heart and lean not on your own understanding; in all your ways submit to him, and he will make your paths straight" (Proverbs 3:5–6 [NIV]).

Could I consider that God made my crooked path straighter? He can't unbend roads completely without interfering with human will. But maybe, even though the road was painful, God tenderly straightened it out as far as He could.

I reread Proverbs 3:5–6 in the Complete Jewish Bible translation for a different perspective.

"Trust in *Adonai* with all your heart; do not rely on your own understanding. In all your ways acknowledge him; then he will level your paths."

Had God "leveled" my path—our path of marriage? We *had* found each other again. Through our journey, we came out stronger individually. We were getting to truly *know* each other, perhaps for the first time in our lives. We were connecting, laughing again, and loving more deeply. What if the journey needed to happen so God could get us where we needed to be *individually* and where we needed to be to progress in our marriage? If so, could I let go of my own understanding and interpretation of the last decade and trust God's way?

I sat there in God's presence, remembering how I'd felt Him before in so many instances. Perhaps I *could* trust Him completely. After all, in the last ten years, He'd made himself known more times than I could remember. What if He *was* "working all things together for good" by leveling paths the best He could without interfering with human will?

A deeper level of assurance swept over me as I thought of the numerous times He came through and was with me.

I remembered being a child and talking with Him under our backyard lemon tree.

I recalled the miracle of being placed into a faith-based school, despite the fact that my mom and dad served two very different religions, and both of them agreed upon sending me to a nondenominational school—where I met David.

I thought about God's provision in my business and growing my income in a time of impossible odds.

I closed my eyes and recollected a very dark and lonely night when I was alone in my bed and felt God's peaceful presence hovering over me. I kept hearing God whisper, "Stay put. I am with you." I could almost feel His supernatural hand upon me, keeping me there and instilling His peace.

I looked back at God's divine protection during the open house attack.

More memories flooded my mind, reminding me of times I'd forgotten from my childhood, adolescence, and into my adult years— all times where he leveled my path and was with me. And these were only the ones I knew about. I'd bet there were many other times of His presence and shelter I hadn't realized.

Gratitude swirled in my heart. "Thank you, Lord, for your presence, provision, and protection in my life."

I saw anew, as if peeking into the spiritual realm, and began to understand more fully that there were more facets to this three-dimensional temporal world. Every event in my life had to play out the way it did so He could get me to the place He desired for me. I exhaled in relief as I opened my heart to trusting God more deeply and accepting what transpired.

Prior to this, I couldn't let go of the "what ifs." But I learned that living in the "what ifs" and "if only" wasn't a realistic picture of how things actually turned out. No matter how you rationalize it in your mind, chances are it wouldn't have played out that way.

Let go of how you imagine it might develop and trust that you made the best decision you could with the tools you had at the time. And at some point, you just have to trust again—God, yourself, and others.

I took the power back from dwelling in the past and thought about my journey in new ways. When I glanced backward, I reminded myself, "Okay, that didn't go as planned. Next time, I'll do that more skillfully." It brought me back to the present, and I could remind myself of all the ways I've grown for the better.

Living in the present—not dwelling on the past or looking too far into the future—was where I found God's presence. He'd never left; I had.

Acknowledging

A twelve-year-old's time in the spotlight had been rehearsed and prepared way in advance before she stepped onto the stage for "America's Got Talent." Her moment arrived as she started singing.

But all was interrupted when Simon Cowell yelled, "Stop!"

The music faded, and I thought to myself, *What's he doing? She sounds so amazing.*

But Simon Cowell said, "I don't think this backing track is working for you. It's horrible."

Sweet Ansley stood on the stage, not knowing what to say.

Simon continued. "I don't think we can properly judge you on this. I really don't. We like you, but that was terrible. I'm just wondering if we should do a verse and a chorus a cappella?"

Ansley replied, "Umm?"

"Do you want some water?" they asked her.

"Uh, yeah."

She met Simon at the edge of the stage, reached out for the cup, took a sip, and walked backstage to place it out of view. While returning to the center of the stage, she said something that made my heart pause. I almost missed it because I was caught up in her adorableness.

She said, "Okay…uh…um…Well, that just happened."

Before I could process what God was speaking to my heart, Simon said, "Okay, let's do it." She closed her eyes, centered herself, and took a few breaths. The audience cheered as Simon encouraged her. "Come on. You can do this, Ansley."

She closed her eyes again and took another breath while placing a hand on her chest. One of the female judges said, "You got this, girl."

Her mom yelled, "You can do it," from backstage.

She took another breath and waved her hand in front of her face to get more air or perhaps dry incoming tears. And then, she sang. And she nailed it.[19]

Sometimes, God halts life's backup music so we can sing a cappella. After hearing Ansley sing without music, she sounded even better than she did with it.

---

19. *America's Got Talent*, "Ansley Burns: 11-Year-Old FIGHTS On After Simon Stops Her! | America's Got Talent 2019," YouTube, June 18, 2019, entertainment video, 02:23 to 04:56, https://www.youtube.com/watch?v=8SfrccLSHIM.

When God removed my comforting backup melody, I was far from composed. While we need time to gather ourselves and recover from the hurt, sickness, temptation, or grief, we can allow healing by utilizing Ansley's words: "Well, that just happened." We recompose ourselves and move forward with our new life song. God knew my backing track wasn't working for me, so He asked me to sing solo.

Please don't hear me say to use Ansley's words to move on or "just get over it"—rather, hear this: accepting life on its terms is how we receive healing, and it starts with trusting God's plan and bravely acknowledging the situation like sweet Ansley did. By humbly saying, "Well, that just happened," we jump over denial and into the arms of acceptance. It's a way to remain sure-footed during life's rug pulls.

When I admitted, "Yep, that happened," I opened my heart and received what my loving God allowed in my life, and acceptance worked its way in. It didn't fix everything, but it was a solid start.

Emily P. Freeman said on her podcast, *The Next Right Thing*, "Your smile does not betray your heart." In other words, through life's pain, it's okay to take days to smile. As I learned to sing with my new backup track, I also took days to smile when I felt like it. I was healing, learning to self-soothe, and singing the most beautiful song of my life.

"Trust God from the bottom of your heart; don't try to figure out everything on your own. Listen for God's voice in everything you do, everywhere you go; He's the one who will keep you on track. Don't assume that you know it all. Run to God! Run from evil" (Proverbs 3:5–6 [The Message]).

I was trusting God with all of my soul and not attempting to figure it all out by myself. I moved from spending my mornings in bed, journaling about all the muck I'd been through—and I'd written plenty—and shifted to the bedroom windowsill. Each morning, with hot coffee in hand, I allowed the sunshine to embrace me as I whispered simple words of faith and found myself receiving all that God had for me.

"I seek you, God. I want more of you."

"Help me today. Strengthen me."

"Show me something good in this moment. Help me to set up stones of remembrance."

"Remind me there's a greater plan, and help me to believe it."

"Only you can redeem what was lost."

"You are the great miracle worker; make my story a miracle."

When I asked for help, for faith, or simply shared my gratitude with Him, the peace that surpasses all human understanding would envelop me. The solitude came from trusting Him more and addressing problems together. I was finally singing life's beautiful melody.

And acceptance filled my soul.

Choosing

They were separated. It was too much to take. All that she'd been through—all that *they'd* been through. *Unbelievable,* I thought. It was then that I decided I couldn't be a part of that relationship anymore.

I placed the book down, convinced I wouldn't return to it. After a day of not knowing how the story would unfold, I did go back. It was like staring at a bad accident when driving by. I always tried not to look, but I couldn't help it. And so, I returned to the sad, yet inspiring, story of *Modoc: The True Story of the Greatest Elephant That Ever Lived.* Spoiler alert: I'll be summarizing Modoc's story, including how it ends.

A boy named Bram and an elephant named Modoc were born on the same day. Bram and Modoc developed an inseparable bond that lasted a lifetime. Their deep friendship began in a small German town that was part of a famous circus. The circus was eventually sold, and Modoc was loaded onto a ship headed toward the United States, leaving Bram distraught by the idea of being without his dear friend. He decided he couldn't be without her, so he left his family and all he knew. Bram stowed away on the ship holding Modoc, and they sailed off toward the United States together. And that's just the beginning.

The ship sank in the Indian Ocean, and barely surviving that, Bram and Modoc ended up in the Indian teak forest where they were injured by gunfire and captured. Eventually, they made it to New York where Modoc rose to circus stardom. But Modoc was poisoned, burned in a fire, abused, and lost vision in her eye before she was sold by the circus owner. At that point, she was separated from Bram for years.

It was then that I put the book down. It was too much to handle. How could so many painful moments bare any positive outcomes? Modoc was traumatized from all she'd been through, and I couldn't turn another page. I gave it a day before my heart was ready to press on in the story. So, I picked up the book to try again.

Modoc was sold to someone who didn't care for her—who neglected and abused her. Children threw rocks at her, and she was left tied to a tree in a backyard to waste away.

After many years of abuse by her current owner, Modoc, or more commonly known as "One-eye Mo," was bought for one thousand dollars from an exotic animal rental company in California. She was restored to health and treated well. By a miracle, Bram found her, and they were reunited. Bram was hired to work for the animal rental company and was with Modoc every day. In the years that followed, Modoc became a famous elephant movie star in Hollywood.

There were only a few pages left, so I read on.

After over seven decades and everything Modoc had been through, she was thrown a birthday party—a celebration of her heroic life. Through all of life's trials, Modoc put others first. She saved many in the shipwreck and in the teak forest and protected Bram throughout his life.

A circus tent was erected at the animal rescue, and Modoc was led into the ring. The owner of the animal rescue played the ringmaster and announced Bram and Modoc as they entered.

With a single spotlight, the calliope played, and Modoc danced. *She danced!*

She did hops and skips, waltzes, leg-ups, and knew her routine. Modoc danced despite all she'd been through.

* * *

Hurts, disappointments, and tragedies have a rhythm; you have to decide whether or not to dance to them. Modoc allowed herself to sway to life's music. She chose to allow good to come from evil and made meaning out of it all. She danced as if to say, "You intended to harm me, but God intended it for good to accomplish what is now being done, the saving of many lives" (Genesis 50:20 [NIV]).

Modoc seemed to have a higher spiritual understanding of life's challenges. Facing each one with two words: but God. Could it be that even an elephant somehow knew deep within that everything, even in the face of disaster, has a greater purpose?

What a way to face life head-on! Modoc needed to go through all that she did in order to receive her glory and fame in Hollywood.

And more importantly, imagine her eternal glory for the beautiful example she led.

Isn't that true of our experiences too? Everything that's tragic will someday be made right. Someday—perhaps not until we enter heaven—we'll see things for what they really are. There'll be purpose and meaning, and we'll be able to exclaim, "It was worth it! All of it."

Modoc inspired me to look at life differently—in light of eternity. Her story helped me use my trials to strengthen me. "The past gives us our strength."[20]

For Modoc, it was as simple as *choosing* to dance.

While my own life trials were nowhere near those of Modoc's, they were still traumatic to *me*. I had to make a choice: I could wallow over my life's events, or I could dance because of them. I found acceptance because I knew that my life's story had a very specific purpose. God was shaping me into who I was supposed to be. I, too, gained strength through my own storyline.

"So, to be sad about gaining strength is not very wise, is it?"[21]

There's connection between our trials, finding strength in them, and dancing in the arms of acceptance.

My viewpoint of the past decade had finally shifted. Rather than resenting the trials, I saw them as stepping-stones to a better me. God was training up His mountaineer and watchwoman over her own heart, and she'd made a choice: Trust God through every season of her life.

As new trials came, I'd give thanks *in* them, not *for* them. I'd address and acknowledge them by saying, "Well, that just happened." Then, I'd face each situation with God, choosing to dance and accepting all that came my way, come what may.

---

20. Helfer, *Modoc*, 275.
21. Helfer, *Modoc*, 275.

You can transform life's discord and make it your own harmony. It's simply a matter of how you face them.

Trusting and thanking. Acknowledging. Choosing.

When the calliope plays, choose to dance.

There's hope in God and how He shapes you through each circumstance.

My friend and fellow author, Bill Clarke, said it best. After suffering a stroke at fifty-five years old, he said in his book *My Path to Heaven on Earth*, "I could still play tennis, but I needed to resort to a different style of play."

You and I can resort to a different style of play. That's how we find acceptance.

In that acceptance, we become free.

18

Free to Receive

I always get to where I am going
by walking away from where I have been.
—Winnie the Pooh

I WAS IN A ZOOM MEETING WITH MY CAMERA ON AND UNMUTED. David walked into my office and pointed at his eye.

I thought, *What's wrong with his eye?*

I raised my eyebrows to try to gain some understanding, but I kept glancing at my computer screen to let my business associate know I was still listening to her. She continued talking as I kept gazing at David. He pointed to his eye again just to make it clear to me. Then he pointed to his heart. And then at me. Once again, he repeated the three gestures quickly and silently mouthed the words *I love you.*

I looked into his blue eyes before looking him over.

I admired how handsome he was. Through the decade of trials and drifting apart, I still loved him. But my heart swelled seeing him more mature, a bit weathered from the journey, but more striking than ever.

Some people don't get second chances; I thank God we did.

Our lives hadn't just been restored, but retold. A newer, stronger, yet gentler version of David had come to life, making him more attractive than I remembered. As I gazed at him, he whispered he was leaving for a meeting.

I apologized to my colleague and told her that someone was leaving my office and I needed to say goodbye.

Once my meeting was finished, I took a break to reflect. Not only had David changed for the better, but I was made anew.

I sat at my desk in awe of how far I'd come—how far *we'd* come. I remembered a podcast that I listened to in 2019 (and a blog post I read) by one of my favorites, Emily P. Freeman. She shared how to make the next right decision in your life without experiencing decision fatigue.

I remembered how her soft voice whispered deeply to my soul. Emily's gentle words delivered the freedom to say goodbye.

"The prelude to starting over is often one long measure of good-byes."[22]

Certainly, the past few years had been one long measure of good-byes. I was slowly releasing the past and steadily letting go of my former self.

She also said, "May you be sustained for this new journey. May our Father lift your head and empower you to take one step forward into today. May you embrace this new beginning with your whole heart and stop waiting for something to come along and ruin it. Give this new beginning a chance at life…Father, as we stand at new beginnings and grieve those long goodbyes, teach us what it means to hold on to what we need for the journey and gently let the rest go. You bring new mercies every morning and give us the grace to start over as many times as we might need."[23]

---

22. Emily P. Freeman, "A Prayer for Starting Over," *Emily P. Freeman* (blog), https://emilypfreeman.com/prayer-starting/.
23. Emily P. Freeman, *The Next Right Thing*, podcast audio, 2019.

I felt a tear make its way to my cheek. I'd learned to do just that—hold on to all that was necessary and discover what to receive and what not to. I accepted my new beginning and rejected the fear that something would happen to ruin it.

I let go and felt my heart become free.

All the practices I'd learned through the long stretch of my life had grown deep. Looking back, I had quit receiving the wrong things, and the little girl lost was found. I quit pretending and was brave enough to peek. I'd pulled the trigger on my own life and started being the strong woman I was created to be. I confronted myself in making strong decisions and seeing things more objectively. I embraced the ultimate receive—opening to God's will for my life. I employed seven practical steps to transform myself so I could attain the life I wanted.

I'd established my "bottom line." According to Harriet Lerner, PhD, "A bottom-line position stems from deeply held values and gut-level responses...acting for our self rather than against the other person."[24]

I discovered the power of receiving my own preferences without self-judgment. I shaped my inner person for the better, and each experience pointed me a little more toward Christ. I'd learned that "I'm entitled to my preferences and beliefs, but I'm not entitled to make others live in accordance to them."[25]

That, indeed, was freedom.

I also found that I couldn't promise someone else I'll "never, ever." Instead, making a promise to myself was how it was best kept. When doing this, I made a commitment to who I wanted to be— the woman I strived to become when I looked in the mirror. And

---

24. Harriet Lerner, *The Dance of Connection* (New York, NY: Harper Collins, 2001), 110.
25. Schnarch, *Passionate Marriage*, 176.

because God's Spirit resides in me, when I make a promise to myself, I make a commitment to God too.

I lived the statement, "Knowing our bottom line—that is, the values, beliefs, and priorities that are so crucial to preserving and protecting the self that we will not compromise them in any relationship."[26]

Perhaps God took me through this decade because without it, I'd never transform into who I was intended to be. I was chosen.

Knowing God sent me through this journey, I was able to reflect on my past and decide to see it in a different light.

We can choose how we perceive our circumstances—look through the lens of pain or through the optical of blessing.

Instead of seeing the difficulties, I reflected on how God showed up, how He protected and preserved me. I remembered that time as a sanctuary—a safe place where growth happened in difficult circumstances, where God sheltered me and sprinkled manna on the ground each day. His provision and safety glistened everywhere I looked.

In the face of change, the uncomfortable me became strengthened in the battle; I saw who emerged from the fight—a fortified, wise, and beautiful woman—and I loved her.

I staggered through a desert. I climbed and descended my mountain. That won't be my only adventure. More will come, and I pray future treks will be less painful. But I also pray that God uses whatever methods He deems necessary to continually shape me into His son's image. To open my heart in ways I never thought possible and learn more fully how to receive.

Knowing I'll enter more deserts and scale more mountains, I can walk in peace because each experience opens my heart and

---

26. Lerner, *The Dance of Connection*, 3.

reveals a purer version of myself. The difference is I want to better myself, receiving all that God has for me that'll lead me on my next journey.

I walked over to my office bookcase and pulled out my Bible. It was my lifeline during my journey; it also contained cards David had given me that sustained me over the past few years.

The one he gave me in 2018 was my favorite. It read, "You. Only you. Always you," and then in his own words he wrote, "All I have ever wanted is you."

We'd made it. We both emerged better.

In that moment, I smiled at who I'd become. I completely understood that I could only change one thing: myself.

I chose to dance and make new steps along the way. Those I loved were free to step into my new rhythm.

Make new moves, and change will happen.

Most importantly, I'd wrapped my head around the past decade and finally, my heart.

I ran my finger over the card and whispered back, "All I have ever wanted is *you*, David."

I closed my Bible and finally felt completely free to receive whatever was next in my life.

All that was yet to come.

Trek well, good and faithful servant.

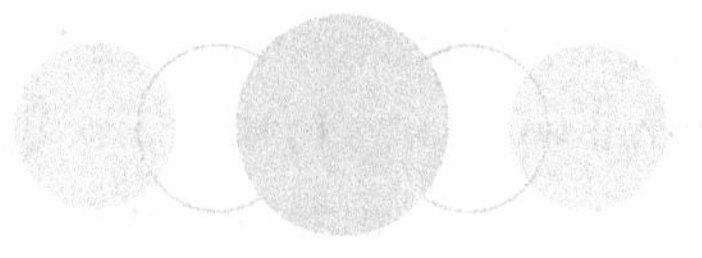

Epilogue

THE WHITE SILK CANVAS OF THE JEWISH CHUPPAH RIPPLED IN the breeze.

Something new filled my spirit—an expectation of what was to come and a strange new sense of curiosity.

Jonathan Cahn was speaking, but my mind drifted to the morning we woke up in the Denver airport hotel. Putting on the final makeup touches, the sense of adventure filled me. In the next few hours, we'd board a plane headed to a strange land. Israel!

David came up from behind and wrapped his arms around me. It was then that I saw it—his wedding ring. How many years had it been since he'd worn it? Years of working with his hands had cracked it, and we'd talked about repairing it, but somewhere along the way, we forgot.

The sight of his hand with the ring on it took my breath away. It was still split, but he wore it anyway. I stared in the mirror at the tattered ring on his finger and smiled at the beauty of the brokenness.

"You're wearing your wedding ring," I said.

"Yes," he replied and hugged me tighter.

There was a solidity and a steady gentleness to him. Aside from our wedding day, that was my happiest moment thus far.

Jonathan's voice sounded in my earpiece, bringing me back to where I really was. "Today, we'll recommit our wedding vows to each other in the land of Cana where, at a wedding ceremony, Jesus performed His first miracle and turned water to wine. If you're single, you can recommit your vows to the Lord. I'll first perform the marriage ceremony and then a time of return to Yeshua. Today is a very special day, so gather around."

The people from our tour group made their way to the front to stand under the chuppahs, but David and I stayed seated at the picnic table at the back of the crowd. In 1989, we had a huge wedding, so I wasn't feeling led to join the masses. Instead, we silently agreed to remain where we were for our own private ceremony.

As instructed by Jonathan, we took each other's hands and repeated after him.

"Arise my love, my beautiful one,
and come with me.
My beloved is mine,
and I am his.
I forgive you,
as you have forgiven me.
This day, I reestablish
my covenant with you.
Do not ask me to leave you,
or to turn back from journeying with you.
Wherever you go, I will go.
Where you dwell, I will dwell.
Your people shall be my people.
And your God shall be my God.
And nothing but death
shall part you from me."

The world melted away as we saw each other for who we truly were and who we'd become. I'm not sure who saw the other's tears first, but we were both moved. Without noticing anyone around, we repeated our recommitment to the Lord—just as the Israelites wandered and returned to God, so had we.

The sacred moment lingered, but not long enough. Our group burst out in a Jewish wedding dance while we remained in the moment. Maya, our tour guide, later gave us a picture she took of us from behind with my hand on David's back—an image that reminds me of God's sovereignty.

There's always hope, so don't lose yours. Receive what God has for you. If you've loved and lost, choose to see that by loving, you've moved closer to the most authentic version of you. If you've never given your heart to someone, at least give it to God. Be true to who you are, love who you are right where you are, and work on receiving a newer and better you.

It's never too late. No matter your age, there's still time to completely become who God called you to be. And nothing is wasted—unless you choose to waste it by not opening up to receive.

When we returned home from Israel, David got his wedding ring repaired. It looked odd, all buffed in shiny new gold. It reminded me how God makes all things new, including each of us.

My heart smiled wide from our amazing trip—not just to the holy land, but to His land of reconciliation. I loved the new me, the new David, and the renewed us. My heart was open to receive the journey and thank God for it—every step of the way.

Acknowledgments

SOME OF MY FAVORITE MEMORIES ARE COOKING WITH MY BELOVED grandma. As a young girl, I'd sit on her kitchen counter and watch her concoct the best meals. She never measured; she created.

Writing sometimes feels like I'm making my grandma's Sicilian spaghetti sauce. My pinch of basil is not the same as hers, and what I crafted is sometimes bland, too spicy, or not brewed enough. Attempting to make something special, I pepper in words, simmer, and adjust. Sometimes it's pretty close. Other times, it's not quite right.

So, when I sent my manuscript to my editors, Daniela, Chrissy, and Jessica, their collaboration helped me find just the right mixture of "seasoning." Thank you, ladies, for turning my simple can of tomato sauce into a well-infused creation. You helped me get out of my head and put onto the page what was truly in my heart.

To my friend and sage, Allen Arnold—thank you for your wisdom and guidance. From the moment I met you, you reminded me to tune out the clamor of agents, publishers, and what others "think I should do" and simply write what God has called me to. Thanks for helping me discover a better way and reorganizing my book. I'm grateful God crossed our paths.

Doctor Laura Mohr, my therapist and search and rescue party, you guided me through treacherous terrain and to an awaiting new dawn.

To the readers who keep me encouraged on the days when I wonder: *Why am I doing this, and does it even matter?* Thank you for reminding me of my gifting, for reading my words, and sharing them with others along the way. You bless me.

My Jericho Girls: Thank you for being my guardrails. You are precious to me.

To my high school sweetie, love of my life, and best friend, David: I wouldn't have become the person I am today without you trekking with me. You have influenced my life and shaped me in ways I would've never known without you. You make me a better human being. If I had to do it over, hands down, I'd choose our thirty-seven-year adventure again.

And to the God of the universe—the great One who reconciles everything and makes all things new—thank you for being by my side and helping me navigate the mountain of my life. May my simple act of writing and creating with you each morning go forth, glorifying you and you alone.

Bibliography

"acquiesce." Merriam-Webster.com. 2011, accessed May 4, 2022, https://www.merriam-webster.com/dictionary/acquiescing.

America's Got Talent. "Ansley Burns: 11-Year-Old FIGHTS On After Simon Stops Her! | America's Got Talent 2019." Talent Recap. June 18, 2019. Video, 0:02:23, https://www.youtube.com/watch?v=8SfrccLSHIM.

Arnold, Allen. *The Story of With: A Better Way to Live, Love, & Create*. 2016.

Brown, Kevin. *The Hero Effect: Being Your Best When It Matters Most*. 2017.

Buffini, Brian. Interview with Alison Levine. *What's Your Everest*. Podcast audio. March 28, 2017. https://www.thebrianbuffinishow.com/whats-everest-043/.

Cuncic, Arlin. "Amygdala Hijack and the Fight or Flight Response." Very Well Mind. Last modified June 22, 2021, https://www.verywellmind.com/what-happens-during-an-amygdala-hijack-4165944.

De Becker, Gavin. *The Gift of Fear*. New York, NY: Dell Publishing, 1997.

EMDRIA. "Experiencing EMDR Therapy." Accessed January 25, 2022, https://www.emdria.org/page/120.

Freeman, Emily P. "A Prayer for Starting Over." *Emily P. Freeman* (blog). https://emilypfreeman.com/prayer-starting/.

Freeman, Emily P. *The Next Right Thing*. Podcast audio. 2019.

Got Questions. "How Many Times Did Moses Ascend Mount Sinai?" Accessed January 25, 2022, https://www.gotquestions.org/Moses-on-Mount-Sinai.html.

Got Questions. "Who was King Lemuel in Proverbs 31?" Accessed January 25, 2022, https://www.gotquestions.org/King-Lemuel.html.

Helfer, Ralph. *Modoc: The True Story of the Greatest Elephant That Ever Lived*. New York, NY: Harper Collins, 1997.

Jewish History. "The Destruction of the Second Temple."
Accessed January 25, 2022, https://www.jewishhistory.org/
the-destruction-of-the-second-temple/.

Lerner, Harriet. *The Dance of Anger: A Woman's Guide to Changing the
Patterns of Intimate Relationships*. New York, NY: Perennial Library,
Harper and Row, 1985.

Lerner, Harriet. *The Dance of Connection: How to Talk to Someone When
You're Mad, Hurt, Scared, Frustrated, Insulted, Betrayed, or Desperate*.
New York, NY: Harper Collins, 2001.

Logan, Bob. *Not Quite What I Was Planning*. New York, NY: Harper
Collins, 2008.

Milov, Alexander, *Love*, 2015, Ukraine, Love Milov, accessed May 4,
2022, http://milova.net/love.

Schnarch, David. *Passionate Marriage*. New York, NY: W. W. Norton &
Company, 2009.

Quote Investigator. "It Is Not the Mountain We Conquer,
But Ourselves." Last modified August 18, 2016,
https://quoteinvestigator.com/2016/08/18/conquer/#more-14308.